Emerging Lives,
Enduring Dispositions

Little, Brown Series on Gerontology

Series Editors

Jon Hendricks
and
Robert Kastenbaum

Published

W. Andrew Achenbaum
Shades of Gray:
Old Age,
American Values,
and Federal Policies
Since 1920

Donald E. Gelfand
Aging: The Ethnic
Factor

Jennie Keith
Old People
As People: Social
and Cultural
Influences on
Aging and Old Age

Theodore H. Koff
Long-Term Care:
An Approach to
Serving the Frail
Elderly

Robert R. McCrae and
Paul T. Costa, Jr.
Emerging Lives,
Enduring Dispositions:
Personality in Adulthood

John Myles
Old Age in
the Welfare State:
The Political Economy
of Public Pensions

Jan D. Sinnott,
Charles S. Harris,
Marilyn R. Block,
Stephen Collesano,
and
Solomon G. Jacobson
Applied Research
in Aging: A Guide to
Methods and Resources

Martha Storandt
Counseling and
Therapy with
Older Adults

Albert J. E. Wilson III
Social Services
for Older Persons

Forthcoming
Titles

Linda M. Breytspraak
The Development
of Self in Later Life

Carroll L. Estes,
Lenore E. Gerard,
Jane Sprague Zones,
and James S. Swan
Political Economy,
Health, and Aging

Emerging Lives, Enduring Dispositions

Personality in Adulthood

Robert R. McCrae
Gerontology Research Center, NIA

Paul T. Costa, Jr.
Gerontology Research Center, NIA, and
The Johns Hopkins University

Little, Brown and Company
Boston   Toronto

Library of Congress Cataloging in Publication Data

McCrae, Robert R.
  Emerging lives, enduring dispositions.

  (Little, Brown series on gerontology)
  1. Adulthood. 2. Personality. I. Costa, Paul T.
II. Title. III. Series.
BF724.5.M38 1984   155.6   83-23862
ISBN 0-316-15763-5
ISBN 0-316-15764-3 (pbk.)

Library of Congress Catalog Card Number 83-23862

ISBN 0-316-15763-5

ISBN 0-316-15764-3 {pbk.}

9 8 7 6 5 4 3 2 1

ALP

Published simultaneously in Canada
by Little, Brown & Company (Canada) Limited

Printed in the United States of America

The longitudinal studies of personality on which this book is chiefly based have resulted from the collaborative efforts of a number of distinguished researchers and thousands of dedicated volunteers. We have benefited most directly from the generosity and commitment of the men and women participants in the Baltimore Longitudinal Study of Aging (BLSA). This book is dedicated to all of them.

Foreword

Where is it? In each of the billions of cells in our bodies? Or in our minds? Then, again, perhaps it is something that happens *between* people. Ought we not also take a look at the marketplace as well? And at the values expressed through our cultural institutions? Undoubtedly, the answer lies in all these factors—and more. The phenomenon of aging takes place within our bodies, in our minds, between ourselves and others, and in culturally defined patterns.

The study and analysis of aging—a burgeoning field—is deserving of an integrated spectrum approach. Now, Little, Brown and Company offers such a perspective, one designed to respond to the diversity and complexity of the subject matter and to individualized instructional needs. The Little, Brown Series on Gerontology provides a series of succinct and readable books that encompass a wide variety of topics and concerns. Each volume, written by a highly qualified gerontologist, will provide a degree of precision and specificity not available in a general text whose coverage, expertise, and interest level cannot help but be uneven. While the scope of the gerontology series is indeed broad, individual volumes provide accurate, up-to-date presentations unmatched in the literature of gerontology.

The Little, Brown Series on Gerontology:

—provides a comprehensive overview
—explores emerging challenges and extends the frontiers of knowledge
—is organically interrelated via cross-cutting themes
—consists of individual volumes prepared by the most qualified experts

—offers maximum flexibility as teaching material
—ensures manageable length without sacrificing concepts, facts, methods, or issues·

With the Little, Brown Series on Gerontology now becoming available, instructors can select the texts most desirable for their individual courses. Practitioners and other professionals will also find the foundations necessary to remain abreast of their own particular areas. No doubt, students too will respond to the knowledge and enthusiasm of gerontologists writing about only those topics they know and care most about.

Little, Brown and Company and the editors are pleased to provide a series that not only looks at conceptual and theoretical questions but squarely addresses the most critical and applied concerns of the 1980s. Knowledge without action is unacceptable. The reverse is no better.

As the list of volumes makes clear, some books focus primarily on research and theoretical concerns, others on the applied; by this two-sided approach they draw upon the most significant and dependable thinking available. It is hoped that they will serve as a wellspring for developments in years to come.

Contents

Emerging Lives,
Enduring Dispositions

Chapter

1

Facts and Theories
of Adult Development

Suppose for a moment that people consulted life-span developmental psychologists as they do fortunetellers—to get a glimpse of their own future. What would we tell them to expect as they grow older? Are there predictable crises ahead? Are they likely to continue to mature and grow, or is it all downhill from here? Will their basic natures and temperaments remain pretty much as they are, or will internal unfolding or changing circumstances (such as wars, illness, or technological innovations) shape new personalities? Do married couples grow apart with the years, or do they come to resemble each other in personality as they sometimes seem to do in appearance?

If asked to make these kinds of predictions for individuals, we would hedge—and properly so. We would point out that the scientific study of adulthood is very young, and little is known with certainty. Only in the past two decades have a substantial number of investigators been active in the field, and these have succeeded mainly in framing useful questions, not in giving definitive answers to them. We would also emphasize that science is concerned with generalizations, not specifics. Epidemiologists, for example, can tell us the life expectancy of the average man or the average woman and some of the factors (such as smoking and exercise) that influence longevity; but they certainly cannot predict the age of death for any particular individual. Too many people smoke and drink and live to ninety and too many athletes die young to allow anything more than statements of probability.

But individuals inevitably apply these statements to themselves. When Gail Sheehy (1976) published *Passages*, tens of thousands of people read the book, not because of a disinterested curiosity about

1

human development or because they admired her prose style (engaging as it was). People read *Passages* because they wanted to make sense of their own past, present, or future lives. It is really impossible to prevent people from applying—or misapplying—scientific generalizations to themselves, and the conscientious scientist will want to make doubly sure that the principles he or she offers are really correct, at least in general.

It is for this reason that we will devote more than the usual amount of space to an examination of the empirical evidence on aging and to the logic of its interpretation. We will consider the problems of distinguishing aging from generational and time-of-measurement effects, the validity of self-report methods of assessment, the adequacy of a trait model of personality, and the advantages and dangers of interviews as a source of data on personality. At each step we will weigh the evidence carefully, taking into account both strengths and limitations. We can state our point of view in a few paragraphs, but a critical examination of it will require the whole book.

The Pendulum of Opinion

When psychologists first asked themselves what happens to personality across the life span, they found a great deal to say about infancy, childhood, and adolescence. Most assumed, however, that adulthood was the endpoint of personality development. William James (1890), in a now-famous dictum, claimed that by age thirty character was "set like plaster." Freud wrote volumes on the first few years of life, but almost nothing on the later years; certainly they held no major role in his theory of personality. The parallel to other forms of development seemed obvious: by age twenty the vast majority of men and women have reached their full height, and, though they may settle a bit over the years, the tall remain tall, the short, short. The same seems be true for certain kinds of intelligence. Why should we expect anything different in the case of emotionality or interpersonal warmth or imaginativeness?

Over the years theorists and observers of adult development found a number of reasons for expecting something different, and they began to outline theories of how people change and why. Changes in health and sexual drive, major role shifts, impending death, and the accumulation of experience might all affect personality during adulthood. Social changes could also be expected to play a role in all facets of aging. Over the past two decades, the study of the relations of personality to aging has become a specialty in gerontology and the subject of serious scientific study and popular literature.

Words like *growth, change,* and *development* brought a ray of hope to those who saw only decline and death in aging. In the 1960s, when people vowed to save the world, and in the 1970s, when they tried to save themselves, the human growth movement encouraged us to look for personality development in adults. Thus there were both scientific and personal reasons for expecting change across the life span.

But it is the nature of science to be self-correcting. Not only did scientific ideas generate theories of adult development; they also led to research. Instead of talking about what might be, or about what we want to be, we can use the research efforts of the past forty years to see what really is going on. More and more, we believe, the findings are building into a pattern, and the pattern is one of stability. Maddox (1968) showed that well-adjusted elderly people remained active. Havighurst and his colleagues (1979), who studied professional careers, were led to formulate continuity theory. Recently Neugarten has propounded the notion of *age irrelevance* to account for the fact that age is not a very useful predictor of social functioning. As we shall see later, within the field of personality research this emphasis on stability has been strongly seconded by the work of investigators like Jack Block (1981). It is beginning to look as if James and Freud were right.

But if nothing happens with age, why write a book?

This reaction is shared by some of our colleagues in the field and is one with which we have often confronted ourselves. One answer would be to persuade people about stability, to disillusion those who are looking for some magic transformation with age, or to reassure those who fear that they are in for a life of developmental crisis and turmoil and would much prefer to get about their business.

There is also another, better answer. We have not said, nor will we say, that nothing happens in adulthood. People live most of their lives in this period; they begin careers, raise children, fight wars, and make peace; they experience triumph and despair, boredom and love. Old age too has its share of new experience and new perspective on the old experience. All of this makes a fascinating story. From our point of view, it is all the more fascinating since one of the keys to the story is the individual's personality. People stay much the same in their basic dispositions, and these enduring traits lead them to particular and ever-changing lives.

A Note on Psychotherapy

An account of some of our research published in the popular press was headlined, "Your personality—you're stuck with it" (Hale, 1981). As clearly as anything else, that phrase illustrates how our research is often seen and why it is generally unpopular. Our findings seem to be read as a sentence of doom for all people who are unhappy with themselves. But the findings do not necessarily mean that at all.

We hope to show in the remainder of this book that the process of aging in itself does not bring about regular changes in personality and that most people change little from age thirty to age eighty in some of the central aspects of their social and emotional makeup. Most people do not change—but that does not mean they *cannot* change.

It does suggest, however, that the change will not come of itself nor will it come easily. Effective psychotherapy or major life experiences (like war or religious conversion) may profoundly alter us, but usually only if we are ready for a change and willing to work to make it happen.

What is "effective psychotherapy"? Each major school of therapy is able to claim its own victories (for example, Rogers and Dymond, 1954; Stuart, 1977), though critics (Eysenck, 1952) have questioned the value of all conventional methods. A resolution of this question would require a volume in itself, and we will not address it here. However, it is worth noting that virtually all psychotherapists would agree that real change in personality cannot be achieved at all without intensive and generally long-term efforts by skilled professionals who create very special circumstances and that even then the prospects of success are by no means certain.

In Search of a Phenomenon

Most sciences start with a phenomenon and try to explain it. Astronomy arose to account for the regular changes in the moon and stars. Biology tries to explain why different species exist and adapt so differently to their environments. Cultural anthropology was stimulated by the puzzling customs of preliterate societies, and abnormal psychology by the bizarre behavior of the mentally ill. But if we ask what students of aging and personality are trying to explain, we are likely to draw a blank. The field of adult personality development seems to have emerged as an afterthought, a logical extension of other branches of study.

Some researchers came to it by way of gerontology, the study of aging. We know that there are major changes in physiology with age, and the popular belief that old people begin to lose their memory has been confirmed by controlled longitudinal studies (Arenberg and Robertson-Tchabo, 1977). By analogy, some investigators began to wonder about personality. Does it too change with age? Is there a gradual decline in emotional or social functioning? Do older people become increasingly susceptible to mental illness, as they do to physical illness?

Researchers who began as students of personality had a somewhat different basis for their questions. We know (or think we know) that there are changes in personality in childhood and adolescence. Infants become emotionally responsive to familiar faces only at about thirty days; at eight months they are likely to develop separation anxiety when taken away from their parents. Middle childhood is a period of compliance for most children; adolescence is generally conceded to be a period of rebellion and turmoil. Data show that self-esteem is usually low in this period and rises as people reach young adulthood (Bachman, O'Malley, and Johnston, 1978). Recklessness and sensation-seeking also seem to decline after adolescence (Zuckerman, 1979).

These observable changes led to theories of child personality development, of which Freud's is historically the most influential. Psychologists trained in this tradition began to ask if the same kinds of developmental changes could be taking place in adulthood. If there were oral, anal, and genital stages in childhood, might there not be later psychosexual stages for adults?

This investigation by analogy or extension is in the highest tradition of science. Physicists look for (and find) subatomic particles that in some respects parallel known particles. Cognitive psychology has benefited from computer models. Often this procedure can refocus common sense and allow us to "see" phenomena we have never noticed before, but which are obvious once our attention is called to them. The discoveries of life-span development may be equally convincing once they are made (indeed, we think they are).

The fact that aging and personality is a field in search of a phenomenon is itself an interesting phenomenon. What it seems to mean is that the changes in personality that occur in adulthood—if there are any—are less dramatic than those of childhood. There are some stereotypes of old and young people, but these are notably inconsistent. Romantic idealism is thought to be characteristic of the young, but what about Don Quixote? Age purportedly brings a mellowing of the spirit—except to cranky old men. Old people are supposed to be more conservative than young, but in China a generation of old radicals was recently ousted from power by a generation of middle-aged moderates.

We can agree that old people are less healthy than the young and that they lose their hair, teeth, and hearing. We cannot seem to agree that they become more or less emotional, sociable, imaginative, or sensitive. The field of aging and personality was intended to answer such questions.

One possible explanation for the lack of common sense ideas about personality change in adulthood is that there *are* no changes. But before we jump to that conclusion, we must bear in mind the particular problems that common sense has in formulating ideas about aging. In order to detect a pattern, we have to see a phenomenon repeatedly. Some parts of what we see are due to chance, some to an underlying regularity, and only repeated observations can tell which is which. The parents of a first baby are concerned with every change, not knowing what is normal development and what might be a sign of illness. By the third or fourth child, however, the pattern is familiar, and the experienced mother is something of an expert in child development.

But we do not live long enough to have repeated experience with adult development. We know our grandparents as old people, but we do not know what they were like as children. We can watch our parents grow old, but it is difficult to separate our own maturing perceptions from real changes in them. We can, of course, observe our own life and the lives of our friends, but we could expect to draw conclusions then only at the end of our lives. And we have grown up in a particular period of history whose twists and turns, rather than aging itself, may have made us what we are.

In short, common sense does not have the distance, or perspective, from which to grasp any facts about adult development except the most obvious. Historical biographers, who can compare across the centuries, and anthropologists (Myerhoff and Simić, 1978), who can contrast cultures, can offer some insight. As psychologists, we base our approach on the premise that scientific measurement of personality characteristics in aging people can also provide a basis for answering this question. Quantitative investigations of large samples of people followed over a period of years can detect even very subtle changes with great objectivity. And psychologists have been concerned with issues of personality development long enough that we now have data following the same individuals over the greater part of their lives. This book is based, first and foremost, on the results of those studies. As we interpret them, they point clearly to the conclusion that personality forms part of the enduring core of the individual, a basis on which adaptation is made to an ever-changing life.

It is only fair to warn the reader that the interpretations we make are not universally shared. A number of theories of adult personality development have been proposed, and many researchers believe that they provide a more insightful account of adulthood than the stability view offers. The evidence on which the stability view rests, like all empirical evidence, is open to alternative interpretations, and a number have been advanced. In particular, as we will see in detail in

Chapter 5, there is fundamental division on what exactly is meant by *personality*. It may turn out that what *we* call personality is stable, while what *they* call personality changes. Special attention will have to be paid to the issue of defining and measuring personality.

For these reasons, a brief introduction to theories of change is an essential starting point for this book. Readers may want to consult the original sources for more extended (and perhaps more objective) accounts of these theories.

Other Views: Theories of Change

Among major personality theorists, only two made significant contributions to life-span theory: Jung and Erikson. The former left relatively unstructured ideas, but was very influential in turning attention to the later years. Erikson, on the other hand, produced an elaborate and finely articulated theory that has become the basis of considerable empirical work. His theory of eight stages of life is probably the single most important theory of adult personality development.

Jung, it will be recalled, objected philosophically to Freud's emphasis on sexuality. Jung proposed that sexual development was central to personality only in the young, in whom the function of procreation was vested. Past the age of forty there must, he felt, be other sources of growth, other areas of concern to the individual. These were more likely to be spiritual than sexual, and instead of revolving around the social function of procreation, they concerned the individual's relation to self. *Individuation* was the term he coined to reflect the continuing process of self-discovery and self-development which he hypothesized would occur in the second half of life.

One of the key concepts in individuation was a balancing of opposing traits. Jung (1923) conceived of the self as having two sets of opposed functions for dealing with internal and external reality: thought versus feeling, and sensation versus intuition. At any time in the life of the individual, one or another of these functions would be dominant, and its opposite would be repressed. In order for there to be a full and complete expression of the self, however, the repressed side of the personality would also have to be allowed its chance. The psychological ideal was found in old age, when an integration of opposing functions would mark the culmination of development. Similarly, other personality structures, such as the persona and shadow (which represent socially acceptable and unacceptable aspects of the self) and the anima or animus (the feminine side of men or masculine side of women) must also be integrated. In general, this view of adult personality would lead to the expectation that the manifest characteristics of the young person should change markedly with age, either becoming their own opposite or moderating in degree as they were integrated with their complements.

Jung's theories were based on his experience with psychiatric patients and on his own experience of aging, and were buttressed by his scholarly studies of such obscure fields as alchemy and the *I Ching*. Few psychologists have claimed fully to understand his ideas, and few subscribe to them *in toto*, but some of the basic notions, such as continued and personalized development and the rise of repressed sides of self, have left a profound mark on subsequent theories.

Erik Erikson's (1950) views of adulthood, on the other hand, have become received wisdom in all their details. Erikson belongs to the group of ego psychologists (along with Fromm, Horney, Rapaport, and Anna Freud) who began with classical psychoanalytic theory and in greater or lesser degree modified it to take into account features they believed had been slighted by Freud. Psychoanalytic theory is fundamentally biological in tone and leaves little room for the influences of culture or the individual's own efforts at growth and change. Erikson's solution to the problem of accounting for social and environmental influences on personality was to argue that the traditional psychosexual stages that formed the backbone of Freudian personality development were paralleled by psychosocial stages. In addition to oral conflicts, the infant was faced with the resolution of the issue of basic trust versus mistrust, and each person's resolution of this conflict was heavily shaped by the cultural traditions that dictated methods of child-rearing. Corresponding social issues were postulated for anal, phallic, latency, and genital stages.

Having made the transition from sexual to social stages, Erikson found that he was free to extend the social stages beyond the limit of sexual development. He hypothesized that the young adult needed not only genital gratification but also psychological intimacy in order to form the lasting bonds needed for the establishment of family life. He or she was required to resolve the crisis of intimacy or be left with a pervading sense of isolation. In the period of child-rearing and adult careers, a new issue—generativity—became salient. Individuals who do not adopt an orientation that fosters growth in their children and community succumb to a sense of stagnation and meaninglessness. Finally, in old age the approach of death and the completion of life tasks leave the individual with the realization that his or her life is over and that there will be no second chances. Poorly resolved, this crisis leads to bitterness and despair; well resolved, it brings about a sense of ego integrity and an acceptance of both life and death.

Erikson's model of development is epigenetic, which means that the resolution of each crisis depends on the outcome of former resolutions. The best preparation for ego integrity is a life marked by intimacy and generativity (as well as desirable outcomes of the crises of childhood). But Erikson also admits a considerable element of changeability: at each crisis there is a possibility of new success or failure. The opportunity to redeem a misspent life at any age is one of the more inviting aspects of this theory.

Most of the empirical research on Erikson's stages has been confined to the period of adolescence and the transition to adulthood (for example, Constantinople, 1969; Whitbourne and Waterman, 1979), but occasional studies have also been conducted on middle-aged and elderly people. Erikson's ideas have been more widely adopted, sometimes in modified forms. Certainly the notion of stages of adulthood has become widespread, and the conception that orientation to life must change with point in the life course seems unquestionable. [As Neugarten (1968) notes, at some point in middle age life begins to be measured in terms of time left to live rather than time lived.]

After the 1950s research took the place of theorizing in this area. Even earlier one investigator had made significant contributions to the literature. Charlotte Bühler (1935) examined diaries and other personal records to chart the course of life in substantial samples of people. She noted a general "curve of life" including periods of growth, maintenance, and decline, and focused on the motivational changes that she believed occur with age. For the young person instrumental strivings are central to daily activities; for the older person they become much less important and are replaced by concerns for intrinsic values.

A large number of empirical studies were undertaken, in some cases to test the theories proposed by Erikson and Jung, in others simply to see what happened as people aged (Neugarten, 1977). Cross-sectional comparisons of young and old on a plethora of variables were conducted, retrospective accounts were collected from aged men and women, and a handful of longitudinal studies were launched. We will return to these studies in later chapters; they do not concern us here since they did not lead, in most cases, to theories of adult change. A few regularities were reported from the cross-sectional studies, including an increase in the level of introversion with age, but this change was rarely interpreted.

An exception to the atheoretical bent of these researchers is found in the work of Neugarten and her colleagues. At least two significant theoretical concepts of change in adulthood emerged here, based in both cases on research using the Thematic Apperception Test (TAT), in which psychologists interpret the stories told by subjects in response to a standard set of pictures, some commonplace, some bizarre. Neugarten herself (1964) is responsible for the concept of interiority. She postulated that older individuals turn inward and consolidate their sense of self. The identity that the adolescent takes on and the adult acts on is further distilled in old age, and individuals become more and more like themselves. An increase in social introversion reported in some cross-sectional studies is sometimes taken as evidence of increased interiority, but even Neugarten (1968) admits that there seems to be no regular change in social and emotional functioning with age. Some intrapsychic process, not readily observable to an outsider, must be meant by interiority.

Similarly, Gutmann's (1964) concept of ego mastery styles is tied to intrapsychic changes inferred from TAT responses. Gutmann finds evidence in his TAT stories for three styles of mastery: active, passive, and magical. The first is seen in stories that show the hero taking forceful action to solve problems; the second is inferred when the hero accepts conditions as they are and adapts to them; the last, magical mastery, is seen in stories in which the hero distorts the situation or fails to see obvious dangers and problems. A magical solution has lost contact with reality.

Gutmann proposes that there is a universal developmental sequence in mastery styles. Young men use active mastery; middle-aged men, passive mastery; and old men, magical mastery. Originally found in a sample of men from Kansas City, the same pattern reappears, according to Gutmann (1970, 1974), in rural Mexicans and in the Highland Druze of Israel. A somewhat different pattern is found in women, a tendency to use passive mastery appearing in young women and active mastery in older ones. The crossover of the sexes is interpreted as change in masculinity-femininity, somewhat in conformity with Jung's notions of balancing. As women age, they become more masculine in mastery style; as men age, they become more feminine.

It is imperative to note that an ego mastery style is the hypothesized basis for *experiencing* events; it is not the basis for overt action. Gutmann points out that among the Druze the oldest men are the Elders, who have great power in decision making and are vigorous and decisive in running their community. The significance of a magical mastery style is thus far more subtle than it might at first seem. The discrepancy between the overt and observable and the unconscious, intrapsychic, or inferable has bedeviled personality psychology from the beginning; interiority and ego mastery styles are simply the gerontological version of far more pervasive perplexities.

In the 1970s two major theories of adult development were generated at about the same time. (Sheehy's *Passages* was based on early formulations of them.) Levinson and his colleagues (1978) wrote on the *Seasons of a Man's Life*, while Gould (1978) called his work the study of *Transformations*. Both hold that there are distinct stages of personality development in young and middle adulthood, but the differences between the two theories are as notable as the similarities.

Levinson and his co-workers gave intensive interviews to forty men—ten executives, workers, biologists, and novelists. In cooperation with these subjects, the researchers wrote a biography for each man that focused on changes in what Levinson calls the life structure. The life structure includes personality, but it also includes career, marriage, other relationships, values, and so on. According to the scheme worked out by these writers, adult life is divided into fixed and age-related stages. After the early career beginnings comes a period of reassessment at the age-thirty transition. A much more searching reassessment comes at the midlife transition at age forty. In this period, often characterized as a midlife crisis, there is a period of inner turmoil that, according to Levinson, often seems to resemble neurosis. Dreams and aspirations that the young man had repressed in dealing with the realities of starting a career now come to the fore, and often a new career is launched that better addresses the long-denied needs.

Gould, whose version of adult development is more closely tied to personality, devises a version of psychoanalytic thought to explain the changes he thinks he sees in adults. At the heart of the theory is the basic insecurity of the child, faced with the uncertainties and dangers of the world. To cope with these fears, the child adopts a set of beliefs that Gould calls *illusions of safety*. Thus children believe that their parents will always be there to take care of them, that there is no real evil or death in the world, that life is simple and controllable. Each of these illusions is comforting to the child, but each leads the adult to a distorted view of the world. Over the course of early adulthood, individuals must come to terms with these beliefs and abandon them to find a more realistic view of the world.

Gould considers that these illusions of safety, like psychodynamic defenses, are unconscious. The young adult is unaware that he or she assumes that parents will always be there to help—in fact, the young adult may explicitly deny such a belief. But, says Gould, young adults will act *as if* they harbored these delusions, and that is the key to the action of unconscious forces. Becoming an adult, attaining full adult consciousness, depends on outgrowing these illusions, a painful but salutary process. There is, according to Gould, a regular sequence in which the illusions are tackled and thus a rough correspondence to age, but there are fewer chronological absolutes in his system than in Levinson's.

* * *

This review of the major theories of adulthood shows their major strength and one of their weaknesses. The strength lies in the sheer attractiveness of the proposition that individuals continue to grow and change as adults. Surely all the experience of years counts for something! Surely the universal changes in health, appearance, and intellectual functioning have some parallel in personality! Surely there must be some hope for individuals whose current life is not the kind they would want to repeat for the next fifty years!

The first and in some respects the most troubling weakness with the theories is their mutual inconsistency. A number of very thoughtful and insightful observers of humankind have contemplated the course of adult life and have pointed out patterns they seem to see. But these patterns as often contradict as support one another. Gould sees his patients coming closer and closer to reality; Gutmann detects a retreat from reality. Bühler sees the last phase of life as one of decline; Erikson sees it as the time for the development of wisdom. Levinson puts age limits on his stages of adult change; Neugarten hypothesizes a steady increase in interiority. When observers from a dozen different perspectives describe the same phenomenon, we begin to believe it is really there. When everyone reports something different, it is hard to know what to believe. And that is the time to turn away from personal impressions and look at the facts.

Chapter

2

The Search for Growth or Decline in Personality

If we want to know whether personality changes across the adult years, the most straightforward way of proceeding would seem to be to measure personality in young and old people and see if there are any noticeable differences. This simple prescription turns out to be more complex than one might at first imagine. There are several excellent discussions of measuring change and disentangling aging, cohort, and time-of-measurement effects (for example, Kausler, 1982; Schaie, 1977), complete with diagrams and statistical formulas. Our purpose here is not to teach methodology, but to show why a question as apparently straightforward as "Does personality change with age?" is not straightforward at all. We will have to spend one whole chapter on what we mean by measuring personality and two chapters on methods of looking for stability or change. For the present, though, assume that we can measure personality simply by giving standard personality questionnaires (later we will argue that this is, in fact, an excellent way to measure personality). That allows us to turn to the question of whether personality grows or declines with age.

Growth and decline are the most obvious and fundamental of developmental processes. Children grow taller each year until they reach adult stature; thereafter they remain at about the same height for many years, until in old age the settling of bones in the vertebral column makes them shrink somewhat. Many biological functions, notably sexuality, show similar curves, as do some, though by no means all, of the intellectual functions, such as short-term memory and spatial visualization abilities.

Many physical, biological, and social functions, however, do not exhibit the pattern of growth and decline. Some characteristics, like gender or handedness, are established by birth and show no significant change across the life span. Variables of another class go through a period of growth, but show little or no decline. Vocabulary, for example, tends to grow dramatically in childhood and then to level out after the end of formal education, with perhaps very slight increases during the rest of life. Read the novels of old writers (the late Tolstoy, for instance, or Henry James)—there is no loss of words here.

These trends do not exhaust the possibilities. Perhaps growth in personality is unlimited, like the physical growth of some fish. Perhaps the pattern of change is not a simple up or down, but a complicated pattern of peaks and troughs—a possibility suggested by some of the stage theories we have mentioned. Rather than belabor the possible, let us turn to the facts and see if we can simply *describe* the age trends in personality dimensions. Later we can worry about what they mean or where they come from.

Cross-Sectional Studies of Personality Differences

There are some fairly obvious ways of going about looking for this kind of age trend. We can measure an individual's personality now and then return in ten, twenty, or forty years to measure it again. We could then tell what net change, if any, had occurred in the meantime for each individual. This is a longitudinal design, and we will return to it in a moment. The major problem with longitudinal studies is quite simple: they take too long. Few scientists are willing to wait ten years for results, let alone forty. Gardeners may be willing to plant trees now that will not bear fruit for ten years, but few researchers see themselves as gardeners. In fairness, there are some differences. Gardeners know that if they wait patiently they will be rewarded with apples or cherries or plums. Researchers never know what they will find out or if it will turn out to be interesting or informative. If they knew the answers, they would not be asking the questions.

What one really wants is some shortcut method of answering the question of age changes, and the cross-sectional method is invaluable as that kind of tool. In cross-sectional designs one simply takes a group of younger people and a group of older people and compares them on the traits of interest. We might observe that 40 percent of men over sixty were bald, whereas only 2 percent of men under thirty were. Hence, it would seem, baldness is age-related. This is an example of the kind of cross-sectional observation we all make, and it is almost certainly a correct conclusion.

Studies that compare groups of different ages are called cross-sectional because they take a slice at one time of individuals of various ages. Note that this strategy has a number of advantages. For example, if we measure enough people, we can look not only at young versus old, but at much finer groupings: we can contrast people thirty-eight to forty-three years old with people forty-four to forty-nine years old to see if the former are showing signs of a midlife crisis. We can search for a curve of growth and decline by decade or year to say at exactly what point there is a peak in creativity or productivity or depression. In a matter of weeks or months a researcher can estimate the effects of age on whatever variable he or she is interested in studying.

By this method thousands of studies on age and personality have been conducted and hundreds published in the scientific literature. In 1977 Neugarten reviewed the findings that had been reported: egocentrism, dependency, introversion, dogmatism, rigidity, cautiousness, conformity, ego strength, risk taking, need for achievement, locus of control, creativity, hope, the self-concept, social responsibility, morale, dreaming, and attitudes toward aging were all found to be different in different age groups. However, the studies rarely agree with each other: some researchers found that older people are more dogmatic, some that they are less. (Doubtless other researchers have found no age differences at all, but it is sometimes difficult to find a journal that will publish such "uninteresting" results.) Only introversion, according to Neugarten, seems to show a consistent pattern of increase in the latter half of life.

Lawton and his colleagues (1980) reviewed eleven studies that compared young and old people on a widely used measure of personality and mental illness, the Minnesota Multiphasic Personality Inventory or MMPI. These studies suggest that older persons are higher in depression and hypochondriasis and lower in thrill-seeking or impulsive tendencies, rebelliousness toward authority, and suspiciousness. Certainly these conclusions seem plausible, but we will return in a moment to see some evidence of a more plausible explanation for the findings.

Though widely used, the MMPI is not necessarily the best personality measure for all purposes. Originally intended as an aid in the diagnosis of mental illness, it is geared to a population with serious mental and emotional problems and may not be appropriate for a normal group. Fortunately a number of other standard personality inventories have also been used to compare young and old. Eysenck and Eysenck (1969) have reported that young people are more extraverted, but also higher in neuroticism, than older persons. An examination of several other standard measures, including the Sixteen Personality Factor Questionnaire (16PF) and the Guilford-Zimmerman Temperament Survey (GZTS), shows a similar pattern for certain kinds of extraversion—especially in ascendance, or the predisposition to lead or dominate others. Scales measuring various forms of neuroticism (hostility, anxiety, depression, poor impulse control) show a much more mixed pattern. Finally, a few studies have concurred in finding lower scores for masculinity in older men. The results here seem to depend on the measure used: the masculinity-femininity scale of the MMPI does not show age trends, nor does the tender-mindedness scale of the 16PF, which is the nearest approximation to a femininity scale in that instrument. But on the GZTS there is at least some evidence of decline in masculinity with age (Douglas and Arenberg, 1978).

There are several different ways to interpret these studies, and most of the interpretations would be championed by one writer or another. One reasonable reading of the literature would be that there are age-related declines in some aspects of extraversion, but that most other aspects of personality remain constant across the life span; this is in fact the major conclusion of Neugarten. But many researchers in the field are not satisfied with this conclusion. Their inclination is to throw out the entire line of evidence, on the grounds that cross-sectional studies are fatally flawed. Despite the economy and appeal of the idea behind cross-sectional designs, it may be illegitimate to infer age *changes* from age *differences*.

When we make cross-sectional comparisons, we are in effect assuming that the young people of today will eventually come to resemble the current generation of older people. In some respects, such as the increased incidence of baldness, they almost certainly will. But we do not know whether they will also have the same attitudes, the same habits, or the same personality as today's elderly. In short, we do not know whether personality is shaped more by aging or by cohort factors, by intrinsic maturation or by the social history of specific generations of people.

In the early days of personality theory, under the influence of Freud's models of development, it was assumed that personality was formed early in life as the result of a complex series of interactions between child and parents. Overly rigorous forms of toilet training and general discipline were held to be the source of fixations, inhibitions, and neuroses in later life. While Freud himself never advocated such a simple relationship, many psychologists, pediatricians, and educators came to the conclusion that we would all be more emotionally healthy if we were given more freedom as children. Dr.

Benjamin Spock's (1946) immensely influential writings on child care took a step in this direction, and books like Neill's (1977) *Summerhill* showed what childhood could be like in an atmosphere of freedom. Over the past half century, corporal punishment has almost disappeared from schools and has certainly declined in most households. Today, however, many psychologists and educators are calling for a return to firmer discipline, just as Neill tried to distinguish between freedom and license.

The point is not that today's form of discipline is better or worse than that enjoyed by children fifty years ago; the point is that it is demonstrably different. According to the basic tenets of some forms of personality theory, this difference in the treatment of children ought to have the most dramatic consequences for their adult personality. If child-rearing changes across generations and if adult personality depends on child-rearing, different generations should show major differences in personality. These differences, however, would reflect not the action of aging but the accident of birth into a particular generation.

This confusion of generational or birth-cohort differences with age changes is not merely hypothetical. There are a number of documented cases in which cohort differences have been shown to be responsible for cross-sectional findings. Bones in the leg, for example, are typically a bit shorter in older men than younger. This is not a maturational effect, however, but a cohort effect (Friedlander et al., 1977). More recent generations of children have enjoyed better diets and have as a result grown taller in childhood and adolescence. Somewhat closer to the topic at hand, generational differences have also been shown to account for most of the age differences in vocabulary that have been reported (Schaie and Labouvie-Vief, 1974). Most vocabulary is learned in formal schooling, and today's children have much more of that than their grandparents did.

If we return to the cross-sectional studies we have reviewed, we may now want to revise our conclusions. Perhaps the consistent decline in extraversion is due to changing styles of child-rearing. When children were taught to speak only when spoken to, they may have developed lifelong habits of reticence. The formal interactions of children with their parents may have put a permanent damper on interpersonal warmth and spontaneity. Thus the older generation we see now may be more introverted not because of age, but because of what passed for good breeding a few decades ago. Today's outspoken, uninhibited children may turn out to be outspoken, uninhibited oldsters half a century from now.

On the other hand, it is also possible that very different things are going on under the camouflage of age differences. If there are such significant changes in child-rearing, should we not be seeing many and massive age differences when we compare distant generations? Or is it possible that the absence of consistent age differences is the result not of stability but of equal and opposite effects of aging and cohort? This perplexing idea, which plays a central role in many arguments about aging research, deserves a bit more discussion.

Suppose that, as progressives hope, the change in child-rearing practices over the past fifty years has really had the beneficial effects that it was supposed to: suppose that today's young adults are mentally and emotionally healthier than the young adults of 1930. Suppose further that, in the process of living and learning how to adapt, all people tend to grow in mental health with the years and to overcome the handicaps of a less-than-optimal upbringing. Then we would say that society as a whole is getting healthier and healthier, as each new generation starts off better, and as each individual, every day in every way, gets better and better. Note that under this optimistic set of assumptions, there would be little evidence of age differences when cross-sectional comparisons were made: the older individuals would have risen from a level of poor mental health to good mental health, but they would not now differ from young adults whose good mental health is the result of enlightened child-rearing practices. Thus two major effects on well-being—one linked to socialization, one to aging—could jointly give the appearance of "no differences."

Lest the reader be unduly encouraged by this hypothesis, note that the opposite set of premises could yield the same conclusion. Perhaps what we have seen in the past years is the decline of civilization, a breakdown of discipline that leaves each successive generation with fewer and weaker inner resources. If at the same time aging has the same deleterious effects on mental health as on physical health, all of us are getting worse with each passing day. And yet, again, a comparison of young with old people would show equal levels of mental health—or, in this case, mental illness.

Alternative interpretations like these are the despair of social scientists and have prompted many to abandon altogether the cross-sectional study. And there is yet another flaw that has often been associated with it, the problem of biased sampling.

Virtually all psychological research makes use of sampling and statistical inference in reaching its conclusions. We do not give personality tests to *all* eighty-year-olds and *all* thirty-year-olds; we give them to some few whom we can persuade to take them. Yet the conclusions we are interested in are not limited to the group we happen to have measured, but concern aging in general or eighty-year-olds in general. A great deal of acute mathematical thinking has gone into the development of statistical tests that allow us to determine whether the differences we see between two random samples are real or simply a chance outcome of the particular group of people we happened to examine. In general, the larger the sample, the better the estimate of the true score for the population, the whole group about which we want to make generalizations. Samples of about 2,000 are routinely used to estimate the feelings of 200,000,000 Americans on such issues as the energy crisis or the likelihood of an economic depression.

Sampling itself, then, is not a problem for science. The trouble comes in the requirement that the sample be *random*. If we could go through the records of the Census Bureau, selecting every 100,000th citizen, we would be in a good position to make the best of a cross-sectional study. But samples tend to be quite different in real life. In practice, we find a sample by asking the cooperation of a senior citizens' group or by advertising in the paper or by asking our friends if they or their parents would participate in our study. This is sometimes called haphazard sampling, since it is neither really random nor exactly systematic.

In the early days of gerontological research, some dreadfully flawed conclusions were reached because of this problem. Old people were selected from nursing homes, since there were few senior citizens' clubs in those days; young people, of course, came from the colleges at which the researchers worked. The so-called age differences that emerged from these studies painted a dismal picture of old age: the older people were less intelligent, less mentally healthy, rigid, depressed, and so on. The fact that college students represented the elite of their generation, while nursing home residents were by and large the worst-off of theirs, was somehow forgotten. If we were to extrapolate from these cross-sectional findings, we would discover, for example, that by the time we are in our eighties we will only have had an eighth-grade education!

Errors this obvious are rarely made today. But sampling still presents problems, the magnitude of which we can often only guess. Are results biased by the fact that some individuals in a sample have died before their personality was measured? Are older people who would respond to a newspaper advertisement for an experiment relatively more adventurous or curious than young people who respond?

Useful as cross-sectional studies are for finding out a good deal in a short time, they are limited by the confidence we can place in what we think we have found out. In science, as in the marketplace, you generally get what you pay for, and cross-sectional research is bargain-basement gerontology.

Longitudinal Designs:
Tracking Changes over Time

Most of the problems associated with cross-sectional studies can be solved by using the other major method of aging research, longitudinal studies. In these, a group of individuals is selected and measured at one time, then followed and measured repeatedly over a period of years, perhaps for decades. In contrast to the age differences estimated by cross-sectional studies, longitudinal studies estimate age *changes*. That is, they can see directly how the individuals under study have changed and at what point the changes occur. (As we will see, this does not necessarily mean that the changes are *due to* aging.)

The major appeal of the longitudinal design is its ability to separate changes from generational effects. People only live once. They may absorb in their youth the characteristic tone of their generation, but having done so, they retain it for life. Longitudinal changes cannot be the result of generational differences, nor is there much evidence to suggest that individuals of different generations change in different ways or at different rates, at least with regard to personality.

In contrast to the hundreds of cross-sectional studies, there are only a handful of longitudinal studies of adult personality. The reasons should be clear: it is extremely difficult to keep track of people over a period of many years, and the rewards of longitudinal research are remote. In fact, virtually all the studies to be reported demonstrate the altruism of a set of foresighted scientists who began the measurement of personality in studies others would eventually report.

These studies vary considerably in the kinds of individuals studied, the methods and instruments used to measure personality, and the intervals at which measurements were made. They are quite consistent, however, in their conclusions: there is little or no evidence of longitudinal change in personality characteristics in the period of adulthood, from thirty to eighty years of age. Let us turn to some of the specifics.

Stability in the 16PF

Our early research on aging and personality was conducted in conjunction with a longitudinal program sponsored by the Veterans Administration in Boston, the Normative Aging Study (Costa and McCrae, 1978). The participants in this project are 2,000 men, mostly veterans, ranging in age from twenty-five to ninety years. Most are white and long-term residents of the Boston area. Although there are relatively few individuals from the lowest socioeconomic levels, there is a reasonable representation of subjects with a high school education and beyond. Of course, as in all such studies, the participants are volunteers; in this case they have volunteered to return to the clinic every five years for tests. They also complete questionnaires mailed to them at home as the need arises. In addition to medical examinations the men have been given occasional assessments of personality and cognitive abilities. Between 1965 and 1967 about half the participants were given Cattell's Sixteen Personality Factor Questionnaire or 16PF (Cattell, Eber, and Tatsuoka, 1970). This widely used instrument has, as its name suggests, sixteen scales for the measurement of traits that Cattell believes are the basic dimensions of human personality, including assertiveness, imaginativeness, tension, liberal thinking, and tender-mindedness (or femininity).

In 1975 we readministered a form of the 16PF to a group of 139 men, originally aged twenty-five to eighty-two. Among other things we were interested in seeing if there were systematic declines or increases in the traits measured by the 16PF. Of the sixteen scales, two, intelligence and social independence, were significantly higher at the second administration; fourteen showed no evidence of change over the ten-year interval studied. Tension, adventurousness, liberal thinking, tender-mindedness, and conscientiousness—among other traits—neither increased nor decreased for the average man in this sample. In retrospect, we view this as the major finding of the study. At the time, however, we were as curious as everyone else about the changes. The scales that absorbed our attention were the two that changed. But as we examined our findings in detail, it became clear that they were probably *not* the elusive age changes we had been seeking.

In 1975 the participants scored higher on measures of intellectual brightness and social independence. We suspect the increase in intelligence scores was probably a matter of testing. When people are given the same test twice, they tend to do better the second time, even though they are not actually any more intelligent; this is called a practice effect. In addition, the test was given at the laboratory on the first occasion, under timed conditions; in 1975 the men completed the test at home, at their own pace. Allowing more time may have improved scores. We concluded that it was unlikely that the men had actually become more intelligent with age.

The longitudinal change in the social independence scale was more puzzling. For one thing, there were no cross-sectional differences in this trait. That meant that, if real longitudinal changes were taking place, they were not showing up in cross-sectional comparisons because they were somehow obscured by generational differences. It is precisely because of the possibility of such confusions that researchers turn to longitudinal designs; when they find evidence of them, however, it is usually an unpleasant surprise. We were faced with the prospect of explaining not only why individuals became less dependent on the approval of social groups as they aged, but also why different generations (or, as we will see, times of measurement) also influenced this variable.

Before exerting our creativity in looking for an explanation of this curious finding, we should be sure there is really something here to explain. The fundamental principle of science is reproducibility: a phenomenon must be dependable, regardless of how or by whom it is observed. Few phenomena in the psychological sciences show the invariance of the laws of physics, because our constructs are more abstract and less easily and accurately measured. But we have a right to demand that results be generally replicable—that most investigators will report the same general findings and that we can show them ourselves using different measures or different groups of people. The fact is that many so-called findings in psychology are the results of chance, and even the statistical methods that psychologists adopt do not protect them from drawing the wrong conclusions once in a while. One alternative, therefore, is to ascribe the longitudinal change in group-dependence to pure chance. The finding may be meaningless, a fluke.

There is some basis for thinking that this might be so. Social independence is an aspect of introversion, and our finding might be taken as evidence that individuals become more introverted with age—an interpretation that supports some theories of aging. But the 16PF also has several scales that tap other forms of introversion-extraversion, and none of these other scales shows a similar change in our sample. If we wanted to find evidence of change (as many developmentalists do), we might argue that independence happens to be the only aspect of extraversion that shows maturational change. In principle there is nothing wrong with this hypothesis. If all extraversion scales behaved identically, there would not be any reason to measure them separately. But notice that in order to claim this longitudinal change as an age effect, we have to make two rather cumbersome assumptions: first, that the maturational changes do not show up in cross-sectional studies because of some mysterious confounding of generational differences with age changes; and second, that there is something special about independence that distinguishes it from other, closely related scales that show neither the maturational changes nor the generational differences. Possible, but unlikely.

Fortunately, there is a much more direct way to find out if this was a chance result. An independent longitudinal study carried on at Duke

University over a period of eight years also employed the 16PF, although in a slightly shorter, simplified form (Siegler, George, and Okun, 1979). Researchers there looked for age changes and differences in a sample of men and women initially over forty-six years old, who represented not only a different geographical region, but also a somewhat broader range of socioeconomic status. These researchers also reported that their subjects improved on the second testing of intelligence, but they found neither cross-sectional differences nor longitudinal changes in independence. Thus the apparent decline in extraversion is not replicated across methods (longitudinal, but not cross-sectional), facets (social independence, but not other extraversion scales), or samples (Boston, but not Duke). Since replication is the foundation of scientific inference, the case for change in that personality trait seems closed.

The Duke investigators also report an anomalous finding: although there were no cross-sectional differences in guilt-proneness, a scale which measures an aspect of neuroticism, they found that with time men tended to score lower and women higher on this scale. None of the other neuroticism scales showed the same pattern, nor did the men in the Boston study become less guilt-prone with age. Again we conclude that this finding can best be ascribed to chance.

Most importantly the Duke study confirmed the Boston study in finding overwhelming evidence of stability. It found neither age differences nor longitudinal changes in the degrees to which subjects were outgoing, emotionally stable, assertive, happy-go-lucky, conscientious, adventurous, tender-minded, suspicious, imaginative, shrewd, liberal-thinking, independent, controlled, or tense.

The GZTS: Changes over Six Years

In some respects the most thoroughly analyzed data on personality differences and changes come from the Baltimore Longitudinal Study of Aging (BLSA). This program, about which we will have much more to say in the remainder of this book (since our own recent work has been conducted there), began in 1958 to follow a group of community-dwelling men every year or two in order to chart the course of medical and psychological changes with age. The study employed another major personality inventory, the Guilford-Zimmerman Temperament Survey or GZTS (Guilford, Zimmerman, and Guilford, 1976), whose 300 items ask the subject to agree or disagree with such statements as "You find it easy to make new acquaintances" and "You daydream a great deal." Ten scales scored from the responses measure such traits as sociability, activity, masculinity, and emotional stability.

In 1978 Douglas and Arenberg analyzed GZTS data that had been collected over a twelve-year period. We will return shortly to some of their more sophisticated analyses; at present we are interested in the longitudinal changes they found. In contrast to the largely negative findings of studies using the 16PF, Douglas and Arenberg reported that five of the ten GZTS scales showed longitudinal changes. At the second testing six years later, men in the BLSA scored lower on activity, friendliness, thoughtfulness, personal relations, and masculinity. They did not change on restraint, ascendance, sociability, emotional stability, or objectivity. We will undertake a more detailed consideration of these findings after we have introduced yet another complication in methodology and another set of partial solutions.

Sequential Strategies: Avoiding Practice and Time Effects

Longitudinal methods, we have pointed out, are free from some of the problems of cross-sectional studies, but they have other problems of their own. One of these we have already encountered in discussing the changes in intelligence seen in the Boston and Duke studies. When individuals take the same test repeatedly, they may answer differently simply as a result of exposure to the test. When an ability test is in question, this is called a *practice effect*, and that term has also been used to describe other effects of repeated measurement. People may find a personality test less threatening the second time, for example, and give more candid answers. Or they may find it boring and become careless. These differences might show up as "longitudinal changes" when the results of the first and second tests are compared, even though they have nothing to do with the aging process.

On the other hand, some critics have pointed out that individuals often like to give an impression of consistency. They may recall what they said the first time when asked to respond again, and they may try to give the same answers. This would give the impression of stability even in the face of real change.

Test makers are painfully aware of this problem and have come up with a few partial solutions. One is to use a different but similar test the second time—a so-called parallel form. This is the solution adopted, for example, by the Educational Testing Service when students take the Scholastic Aptitude Test (SAT) on more than one occasion. Since each test is different in content, there is no direct possibility of remembering the questions and figuring out the answers between tests. But most students still score a little higher the second time they take the test, probably because they feel more comfortable with the process. Parallel-form testing is not a perfect solution.

If we are really concerned with the growth and change of a particular individual, the problem of practice effects is unavoidable. But if we are only interested in finding out whether people change with age, an alternative strategy has been advocated by a number of prominent developmental methodologists (Schaie, 1977; Baltes, Reese, and Nesselroade, 1977). Suppose we take a random sample of individuals born in 1900 and randomly divide them into two groups. We know from the laws of statistics that, if we have a large enough sample, the two halves are unlikely to be different on any variable we choose to measure; they are equally representative of the population of men and women born in 1900. Next, suppose we measure the personality of the first group in 1960, but do nothing to the second group. If we return in 1980 to measure the first group, we will have the standard longitudinal design, and we will never quite know if the differences we find (or fail to find) are due to aging or to practice effects. However, if in 1980 we measure the *second* group and compare it with the first group as measured in 1960, the difference cannot be due to practice (because the second group has never taken the test) and may therefore be due to aging itself. (Incidentally, if we measure both groups in 1980, we can compare changes for the groups with and without practice and so estimate what the pure practice effects are. That is extremely useful information for other investigators, who need to know whether they should worry about practice effects or whether they can safely ignore them.)

This design, in which individuals born at the same time are measured at two or more different times, is known as a cross-sequential design with independent samples, or, as we will call it, a cross-sequential design. A related design is called time-sequential; here individuals of the same age are measured at different times. Sixty-year-olds, for example, might be surveyed in 1960 and in 1980. The differences could not be due to aging itself, since both groups are the same age. They could, however, be due to generational differences, since the sixty-year-olds of 1960 were born at the turn of the century, whereas the sixty-year-olds of 1980 were born in 1920. A great deal of ingenuity went into the invention of these designs, and they elegantly solve some of the vexing problems of aging research. But they too are ambiguous, for a reason that has not yet been mentioned.

Take as an example attitudes toward women. Suppose we had asked a national sample of twenty-year-olds in 1960 if they believed that women should have their own career, freedom of choice in family planning, or the right to participate in professional sports. Probably few would have endorsed these aspirations. But when we ask the same questions of a different group from the same cohort (now forty-year-olds) in 1980, we can anticipate that a much larger proportion will agree. We know this is not a cohort effect or generational difference, since all these individuals were born in the same year. We know it is not a practice effect, since the respondents in our second sample have never been interviewed before. But surely we would not conclude that it was an aging effect, that individuals adopt increasingly liberal attitudes toward women as they grow older. It is more likely that we would insist the times had changed and almost everyone had modified opinions on these issues as a result of the women's movement. This would be a clear example of what is known as a time-of-measurement effect. Another would be temporary changes in attitudes toward blacks after the assassination of Martin Luther King.

Pollsters are as plagued by time-of-measurement problems as educators are by practice effects. Some theorists (Baltes and Nesselroade, 1972) have claimed that these problems are less crucial to personality investigators, because personality is unlikely to be shifted by temporary historical movements or swings in attitude. Perhaps so, perhaps not. In view of how little we know about adult personality, many would argue that it is not safe to make that assumption. What we need is a design that avoids the problems of the cross-sequential design—one that can compare people at different ages, but in which we can rule out the possibility that time of measurement is responsible for the apparent effect. Is there any way to do that?

There is one way. We can eliminate time-of-measurement effects (and practice effects) if we measure all our subjects once, at one time. Of course, in order to see the effects of age we would have to measure simultaneously individuals of different age groups. And this, lo and behold, is nothing other than the cross-sectional design with which we started. We have come full circle.

This curious circumambulation has bedeviled researchers for nearly twenty years and left the field in some perplexity. A number of additional designs of greater complexity have been proposed to break out of the circle, but astute critics have always been able to weave them back in. The fact is that individuals are always born in one and only one generation, and they always grow older during a certain historical period when things are changing in a certain way and to a certain degree. Short of cloning people to raise them in different circumstances, we find no way out of the dilemma. Time, cohort, and aging are inextricably confounded.

We might at this point abandon all hope and move to another field of study. Alternatively we can adopt a more constructive point of view (Costa and McCrae, 1982). Although there is no way to be sure that we interpret an effect we think we see correctly, there are ways to improve our chances. When we see the same direction and magnitude of an effect in cross-sectional, cross-sequential, and longitudinal studies, for example, it becomes highly likely that a real aging effect has been found.

Let us return for examples to the Douglas and Arenberg study of changes and differences in the GZTS. You will recall that five of the ten scales showed declines in a conventional longitudinal design. But the results of other analyses suggest that only two of these are likely to be aging effects. Thoughtfulness and personal relations shared a pattern of effects in longitudinal, cross-sequential, and time-sequential designs, but not in the cross-sectional analysis. The longitudinal effect may have been due to aging, time, or practice; the cross-sequential to aging or time; and the time-sequential to cohort or time. The one common element in the three designs is time of measurement, so it seems likely that, during the decade of the 1960s, participants became less thoughtful and less trusting of others. This line of reasoning is confirmed by the failure to find any cross-sectional differences in thoughtfulness or personal relations: when everyone is measured at the same time, there are no age or cohort differences.

Friendliness shows a more complex pattern. Like thoughtfulness and personal relations, it declined in the three designs that share time of measurement as an effect. But it also showed a cross-sectional *increase*. Douglas and Arenberg interpreted this as evidence not of maturation, but of long-term cultural change: "successive cohorts and individuals became more easily aroused to hostility and tended to be less agreeable" (p. 745). Certainly we would want to see replications of this finding before accepting it as valid.

But the Douglas and Arenberg study did have the virtue of weeding out spurious age effects from those that are likely to be real. Only two traits survived this screening: masculinity and activity level, both of which declined with age in cross-sectional, longitudinal, and cross-sequential designs, but showed no effect in the time-sequential analysis. Results were just what one would expect if there were maturational changes in masculinity and activity, and the only alternative explanations involved complicated and improbable combinations of practice, time-of-measurement, and cohort effects.

Before admitting that there are personality changes in the traits of masculinity and activity, however, we must answer two questions. Are these findings peculiar to the sample studied in Baltimore, or can they be replicated elsewhere? And what is the magnitude and therefore the importance of the changes?

The evidence for replicability is mixed or unavailable. Since the 16PF does not have a scale for activity level, no comparisons with the other studies we have reviewed are possible for that variable. However, the 16PF does measure a trait called tender-mindedness, which is highly correlated with both gender and other scales of masculinity-femininity. Neither the Boston nor the Duke studies found evidence of maturational change in this scale. If the changes in masculinity found by Douglas and Arenberg are real, they must be changes in some aspect of this variable not measured by the 16PF tender-mindedness scale.

Finally, the changes in both activity level and masculinity on the GZTS are extremely small. For the statistician, the statement that they amount to about one-eighth standard deviation over seven years communicates that point. For others, another comparison may make it more forcefully. We once computed that at the rate of decrease that we observed of 0.41 items every 6.6 years, it would take our older subjects, initially seventy-five years old, 136 years to reach the same level of femininity as the average college woman. Psychologists may speak of the feminization of older men, but the reader should recall that the process would be fully completed only if men lived 211 years!

As this chapter makes clear, the simple question of "What happens with age?" is far from easy to answer. In many areas of gerontology, the separation of cohort, time-of-measurement, and practice effects from true maturational changes may require a lifetime of work. In personality studies the problem is greatly simplified by the nature of the variables studied. No matter how you view it, the only consistent evidence points to stability. With age, adults as a group neither increase nor decrease noticeably in any of the traits identified by major personality instruments.

Implications: Debunking Some Myths of Aging

What does the evidence of stability in personality mean for our view of aging? For some reason, when we say we find no evidence of growth or decline in personality, people hear only "no growth" and regard us as the bearers of bad news. But there is good news here, too. Perhaps it is unfortunate that people do not continue to grow and develop in adulthood, but surely it is reassuring to find that they do not decline. In view of popular and prevalent conceptions of aging, this is by far the more important implication.

In the past few years socially conscious individuals have attempted to create positive stereotypes of aging, reminding us that the aged are revered in many cultures for their experience and wisdom. Octogenarian musicians and actors and artists are showered with honors, and their current productions are uncritically acclaimed. In many respects this newfound respect for the aged is just compensation for decades of neglect. But it often seems that there is something condescending and infantilizing about the status we grant them, as if the elderly needed special consideration. Skinner (1983) noted that the mindless veneration with which the ideas of older scholars and scientists are received reinforces platitudinous thinking and contributes to a decline in creativity.

We might even suspect that many people bend over backwards to think well of the elderly because at a deeper level they fear that age is nothing but decline. There are real losses in physical strength and vigor, in sexual interest, and in certain intellectual abilities, for which it is necessary to make allowances. But there are no significant declines in personality.

We need not worry that we will become crotchety and hypochondriacal with age or that only firm resignation can save us from despair and the fear of death. We need not anticipate increasing social isolation and emotional withdrawal from the world. There is no reason to think that our interests will atrophy or that our values and opinions will become increasingly rigid and conservative.

And just as we need not dread our own future, so we need not pity others who have already reached an advanced age. The elderly are no more emotionally vulnerable or ideologically rigid than anyone else, and giving them special treatment in these areas is unnecessary and probably unwise. Older individuals are entitled to all the respect due any human being, but genuine respect means seeing them as they really are. With regard to personality they are no different from any other adults.

*   *   *

We have spent a great deal of time discussing three studies of age and personality—in part because they are among the largest longitudinal studies that have reported data on a variety of personality traits, in part because they illustrate other studies that have come to the same conclusions. Schaie and Parham (1976), for example, in their report on a large-scale longitudinal and cross-sequential study commented that "within the domain of factors identified in our study, we can with confidence support the stability model" (p. 152).

The objection forming in the heads of the proponents of change hinges on that restrictive phrase: "within the domain of factors identified in our study." Are the 16PF and the GZTS exhaustive inventories of personality, or are they only one part of a phenomenon of much greater complexity? Can we rely on self-reports as a basis for the inference of stability or change in personality, or should we use clinical judgments, inkblot responses, peer ratings? The next chapters are concerned with these issues and with the broader questions of what personality is in the first place.

Chapter

3

A Trait Model
of Personality

Our discussion of the problems of research on aging may have left the impression that there is general agreement on the nature and measurement of personality. Nothing could be further from the truth. Gerontologists are much more in agreement with each other than personologists have ever been. Although the situation now seems to be improving, as recently as ten years ago some of the most fundamental principles of personality psychology were forcefully called into question, and there was a widespread belief that personality as a field of psychology was on its last legs.

If we held the same skeptical view today, we would certainly not be writing this book. The developments of the last few years have been little short of spectacular: personality psychology has had a renaissance, with major advances in a number of fields. Life-span developmental psychology has made a major contribution to the rebirth by demonstrating the reality and significance of enduring dispositions.

The renaissance has been made possible only by a reformation in theory and research. Personologists have had to abandon many of their favorite concepts and adopt more realistic if less glamorous ones. The dimensions of individual differences may be less appealing than the vicissitudes of unconscious instincts, but they also have more to say about human nature. (As this book shows, life-span developmentalists are beginning to learn the same lesson: complex and inviting models of psychosocial adult development are far less well established than the simple stability model in adult personality.)

Clearly an entire volume could be devoted to the state of personality psychology today. At best, this chapter can give some sense of the issues and an outline of the arguments we think make a case for a particular model of personality. The model we will develop is central to the remainder of the book, for when we say personality is stable, we mean personality as defined by that model. We will also touch on the issue of personality measurement, since measures and their interpretation allow us to check theories against the facts. We will offer our preferred theories, models, and methods in this chapter, but we realize that our preferences will not be universally shared. The issues we raise here will not be put to rest—indeed, they will recur throughout the remainder of the book.

The Three and a Half Models of Personality

As every student of personality theory knows, three major schools of psychology have been reflected in theories of personality: psychoanalytic, behaviorist, and humanistic. Psychoanalytic theories of personality (Freud, 1933, 1938) stress the individual's unconscious motivations, which must be inferred from such indirect sources as dreams, slips of the tongue, and fantasies. Behaviorist versions of personality theory (Dollard and Miller, 1950) limit themselves to observable behavior and invoke situational determinants, expectancies, and histories of reinforcement to explain behavior. Humanistic psychologies (Maddi and Costa, 1972), which arose in reaction to what were perceived as the irrational and mechanistic biases of psychoanalytic and behavioral theories, emphasize humankind's capacity to think, love, and grow. Each of these approaches has made valuable contributions to personality psychology, and we will have more to say about them later, especially in Chapter 5. Our current concern, however, is to draw attention away from them to an alternative approach to personality that we feel deserves more credit than it is normally given.

The major schools have been interpreted as representing three different philosophies of human nature that, for the sake of contrast, are often depicted in oversimplified form. These caricatures of human nature may not do justice to the intricacies of the theories themselves, but they do highlight the basic concerns of each perspective. From the psychoanalytic tradition, we might infer that the individual is basically irrational, driven by animal instincts, with rational control maintained only by the countervailing forces of socially induced guilt and anxiety. From a behaviorist perspective, the individual is seen as less ominous and unpredictable; indeed, human nature is largely or wholly the result of experiences in the social environment that shape and reward certain behaviors. People are reactive, habit-bound, creatures of the environment they live in. Humanistic psychologists endow people with a far more pleasing aspect; love, creativity, and play are thought to be the quintessential features of human nature, and both irrationality and rigidity are interpreted as signs of the destructive influence of society.

How can it come to pass that individuals who look at the same phenomenon—human nature—draw such different conclusions about it?

One possibility that may account for this selective attention to the facts about human nature is that people are different. Freudians hold that man is naturally aggressive, and they have no trouble pointing to infamous examples of the kind of humanity they envision. Rogerians (Rogers, 1961) believe in the capacity for openness and love, and they, too, find exemplars of their ideas. [Maslow (1954) studied such self-actualizing individuals as Abraham Lincoln and Eleanor Roosevelt as a kind of counterbalance to the case studies of patients that had formed the basis of Freudian psychology.] Despite the claim that people are able to transcend their environments, it is all too easy to find individuals who seem to be wholly a product of a history of reinforcements.

For decades the debate has raged about which of these is the true image of human nature. The idea that they might all contain an element of truth is a truism that has captured the imagination of almost no one. But it forms the basis of another school: the psychology of traits or individual differences.

Are people basically selfish? Some are, some aren't.

Are human beings intrinsically creative? Some are, some aren't.

This position, which emphasizes the consistent differences of individuals, has always played a major role in both common sense and academic psychology. Yet from the beginning trait psychology has been regarded as a relatively minor part of personality theory: not a fourth school, but only half a school—a set of personality measures, a few isolated studies, an appendix to one of the "true" schools.

One of the reasons for this is that it has been possible to view individual differences simply as an aspect of an all-encompassing theory. To the degree that each of the schools attempts to account for at least some individual differences, each incorporates the trait model. Classical psychoanalytic theory (Freud, 1938), for example, proposed that the resolution of psychosexual conflicts in childhood and the development of characteristic defenses lead to enduring character traits, such as those typifying the anal personality. Neatness, punctuality, thrift, and cleanliness are often viewed as the outcome of a fixation during the anal-retentive stage of development. Maslow, a representative humanist, defined individual differences in terms of levels of basic motivation. Social learning theorists (Bandura, 1977), the contemporary descendants of behaviorists, might explain characteristics like masculinity or femininity as the result of role-modeling and socialization processes.

In short, every theory of personality is concerned with the differences as well as the similarities between people. But the concern tends to be secondary. Maddi (1980), who reviews the major types of personality theory, discusses individual differences in terms of what he calls *peripheral* characteristics, in contrast to the *core* characteristics that form the heart of personality theory. Trait psychology would seem to be all periphery and no core; why settle for that when other schools promise both?

One reason is that other schools are less than fully successful in delivering a good model of individual differences. Each school leads to an emphasis on certain characteristics, often to the exclusion of others. Freudian theory, for example, is primarily concerned with neurosis and impulse control. It has an elaborate system for de-scribing the varieties and degrees of maladjustment. But it fails to say anything of significance on why some individuals are introverted, some extraverted. Psychoanalysts might well claim that, from their point of view, differences on this dimension are trivial. Other traits are trivial from other points of view. Only a system that grants the first place to individual differences will attempt to provide a compre-hensive list of traits. And comprehensiveness is essential if we are interested in an area like personality and aging. How can we specify what characteristics do and do not change unless we know the full range of characteristics to look at?

Basic Principles of Trait Psychology

In common speech, when asked to describe someone, we gen-erally rely on trait terms. We say that one person is intelligent and aggressive, another is hostile and unimaginative, a third is shy but loyal to close friends. Learning how to use such words properly, as applied both to others and to oneself, is an important part of language acquisition. As naive psychologists, all English-speaking people subscribe to a trait theory of psychology. Personality trait terms are also central to most or all other human languages (Goldberg, 1981), probably because the language of traits is so useful in getting along with other people that every culture has invented it.

As scientists, trait psychologists have tried to go beyond the naive, common sense view of traits. But the best of them, like Gordon

Allport (1937), have also acknowledged the contributions of the natural system. Human beings have been trying to understand and describe each other for thousands of years, and it would be presumptuous indeed to suppose that psychologists could start from scratch and come up with a better system in a few years. Trait researchers have borrowed from the common sense system in two respects: first, trait theories of personality have often begun by attempting to spell out the assumptions behind the use of trait words; and second, trait measures have been based in varying degrees of immediacy on the language of traits that has been built up over the centuries. We will return to that aspect later in this chapter.

Most definitions of traits include the following elements: traits are dispositions or tendencies to act or react in certain ways, they are relatively broad or general in application, and they endure over time (Levy, in press). Implicit in most definitions is the notion of individual differences: people vary in the amount to which they possess or exhibit different traits, and trait psychology is sometimes called *differential psychology*. We know what people are like by comparing them with others. We need to spend a little time on each of these elements of the definition, to illustrate what each does and does not mean. Despite its basis in common sense, trait psychology has given rise to an exceptional amount of nonsense.

Traits are hypothetical constructs; that is, they are characteristics we ascribe to individuals to account for certain consistencies in their behavior. Since there are many different ways to look at this consistency, the traits we identify are to some extent arbitrary. The ten traits of Guilford, the sixteen of Cattell, and the eighteen we measure with our own personality instrument all carve up much the same territory somewhat differently. Most contemporary psychologists hold that both genetic predispositions and early experience contribute to the development of traits. Most would acknowledge that the nervous sytem and other physiological processes are involved in the expression of traits, but would be careful not to be overly concrete. It is unlikely that we will ever find a hormone that accounts for neuroticism, an area of the brain that controls extraversion, or a gene for openness. Instead, these trait names refer to abstract consistencies in the ways people act and experience, and to whatever complex underlying causes are responsible for them.

All the traits we will be concerned with are found in varying degrees in all people; a few people are very high, a few very low, and most average on most traits. The statement that traits are dispositions means that we can expect them to show up in the person's behavior and speech, as well as in such internal states as thoughts and feelings; and the more of a trait people have, the more likely they are to show the behavior it disposes toward, and thus the more frequently we are likely to see it. Similarly, the more the trait characterizes them, the more intensely they act and react in relevant situations. A very gregarious individual really likes to be around people and frequently is. Frequency and intensity of the appropriate acts and feelings are the major signs from which we infer the level of the trait.

We have taken great pains to say *likely*, because traits are only dispositions, not absolute determinants. A great number of other factors go into the choice of a particular action or the occurrence of a particular experience. Gregarious people like to talk, but they normally do not chatter on during moments of silent prayer. Well-adjusted people may not worry much, but even they are likely to be anxious when awaiting the results of an interview or a medical exam. The requirements of the social roles we play, the facts of the current situation, the mood of the moment, and acquired habits all join in shaping the choice of a particular act, word, or reaction.

Everyone who stops to think about it will agree in principle that this must be true. But psychologists have lately been somewhat disturbed by the estimates of how weak personality dispositions can be. According to most of the published literature, personality traits account for only about 5 to 10 percent of individual differences in actual behavior in any specific instance. On the one hand, this fact is properly sobering for psychologists or laypeople who expect that a personality test will tell them how a person is going to react in a particular situation. On the other hand, personality lasts a lifetime, while roles and moods and situations come and go, and the cumulative effects of personality are enormous.

There is a nasty tendency to equate traits with habits. Habits are repetitive, mechanical behaviors like smoking or driving fast or saying "you know" after every sentence. Habits are specific learned behaviors; traits are generalized dispositions, finding expression in a variety of specific acts. Habits are thoughtless repetitions of earlier behavior; traits often lead people to develop entirely new behaviors, often after much thought and planning. Driving fast may simply be a habit, perhaps learned from observing the way friends or parents drive. But if the fast driver also likes loud music and roller coasters and perhaps experiments a bit with drugs, we begin to see a general pattern we can identify as excitement-seeking. The excitement-seeker may spend weeks planning for a trip to Las Vegas—or may decide to go on the spur of the moment. But in either case going to Las Vegas is not likely to be simple habit. In many respects traits resemble motives rather than habits, and it is often unclear whether a disposition like excitement-seeking should be called a trait or a motive. Trait appears to be the broader term, encompassing motivational, stylistic, and other aspects of human consistency.

Finally, traits endure over time. This means that traits are to be distinguished from passing moods, transient states of mind, or the effects of temporary stress and strains. If an individual is anxious and hostile today but calm and good-natured tomorrow, we attribute these emotions to the situation—perhaps pressures at work or a quarrel with a spouse. Only when emotion, attitude, or style persists despite changes in circumstances do we infer the operation of a trait. Measures of personality traits are expected to show high retest reliability when administered on separate occasions days or weeks apart, because traits are characteristic not of situations, seasons, or times of day, but of the individual at a particular point in his or her life.

Note that traits can be enduring in this respect while still changing over longer periods of time or under special conditions. Psychotherapists are in the business of modifying undesirable traits, and there seem to be spontaneous changes in some individuals. As we saw in Chapter 1, any number of theories argue that certain personality changes should occur with age, and although the evidence in Chapter 2 disputed the claim for *groups* of people, we have not yet seen just how enduring enduring dispositions may be in aging *individuals*.

How Many Traits? Which Ones?

Common sense, thoughtfully interpreted, provided the theoretical basis for trait psychology. But when it comes to content, more formidable problems arise that require considerable empirical research for resolution. How many different traits are there? How are they related to each other? How many different words do you need to describe all the important aspects of an individual's personality?

The English language provides an embarrassment of riches to the personologist who wants to systematize traits. So important are descriptions of people that thousands of different terms have been adopted, distinguishing minute shades of meaning that delight the poet and confound the simpleminded psychologist. Can't we combine synonyms and come up with a more workable number than the 18,000 trait names that Allport and Odbert (1936) found in an unabridged dictionary?

A few people have tried and have offered smaller lists of traits that purport to contain the essence of the psychological distinctions embodied in the English language. Psychologists, of course, could not rest content there—surely, they believed, with their superior insight trained clinicians and researchers could discern new dimensions of personality overlooked by laypeople. So over the course of the past fifty years, hundreds of personality scales have been written to measure traits investigators believed to be important in describing people and predicting behavior. Among these traits are field-dependence (Witkin et al., 1962), hypomania (Hathaway and McKinley, 1943), and pathemia-cortertia (Cattell, Eber, and Tatsuoka, 1970).

On its face the identification of new traits might seem to be the equivalent of the entomologist's discovery of new species of insects or the astronomer's cataloguing of new stars. In fact, it is something quite different. It is easy enough to tell if a new species of beetle is actually new (and if it is actually a beetle!) from the pictures and descriptions provided by the discoverer. Similarly, an astronomer can characterize a new star by its exact position in the sky. But we cannot pin up specimens of anxiety or personal insecurity or neuroticism or guilt-proneness and compare them, nor do we have a map of the "personality sphere" that we can use to check the location of a new trait. How do we know whether the traits that have been proposed are really new discoveries or simply fancy new names for old traits like sociability or fearfulness?

The only way we can tell if a scale measures a totally new trait or is merely some variation on an old one is by measuring a group of people on the proposed new trait as well as on all the older, known traits and seeing whether the measures of the new trait really give us some new information. (The technical name for this process is *discriminant validation*.) Since there are hundreds of new traits and thousands of English language trait names, it is virtually impossible to measure an adequate sample of people on all of them and so settle the issue once and for all. But if we piece together all the research of the past fifty years in which a few traits have been measured jointly and compared, we can begin to see the outlines of the forest we are in. And once we have some notion of the major groups of personality traits, it becomes much easier to judge the contribution of new candidates. In short, we will have begun to map out the territory of personality and to obtain the equivalent of the astronomer's map of the heavens and the entomologist's taxonomy of insects.

This accomplishment has been the goal of a number of major personality psychologists. Allport aimed at it in his list of common-language trait-names. Cattell (1950) deliberately set about the task and even claimed to have come up with the solution thirty years ago. Gough (1957) created an instrument to measure the traits he felt were embodied in folk psychology, and Block (1961) headed a team of psychologists, psychiatrists, and social workers who tried to capture the essentials of their professional knowledge in a set of one hundred personality descriptors.

Not surprisingly, each of these writers has offered a different "complete" system, and a fair amount of research has aimed at sorting out the competing claims. It would be misleading to say that all parties now agree, but a certain consensus does seem to be forming around a few key elements, and this consensus, after years of disputation, is exciting evidence that real progress is finally being made in personality psychology.

The key to the puzzle comes from the observation that, however conceived and measured, some sets of traits cluster together. There is disagreement, for example, on whether depression is really distinct from anxiety; but there is also an enormous body of evidence that people who are anxious are likely also to be prone to depression. They are also apt to be hostile and difficult to get along with. In this way we can identify a set of traits, including anxiety, hostility, depression, self-consciousness, impulsiveness, vulnerability, and so on, that all share a common element of psychological maladjustment. Following Eysenck (1960), a British psychologist who clearly identified this package of traits (and observed that they are especially common among individuals diagnosed as neurotics), we call the cluster *neuroticism*.

If we go back to the systems offered by Cattell, Gough, Block, or many others, we find little agreement on what the exact elements of neuroticism are. Cattell offers as candidates *tension, guilt-proneness*, and poor *ego strength*; in Guilford's system, the individual high in neuroticism will score low in *emotional stability, objectivity*, and *personal relations*. But in almost every system we find that a major portion of the traits fall into the category of neuroticism. It becomes possible to compare the results of research using one instrument with research using others by noting that this dimension is common to all.

Once the neuroticism-related traits have been identified, we notice that most systems also contain a number of other traits. Many of these share a common element of interest in people; and the acute observer will note that people who need people are also likely to show certain other characteristics, such as energy, cheerfulness, and the need for excitement. Again following Eysenck, we call this second domain *extraversion*.

[There is some linguistic confusion here. C. G. Jung first brought to prominence the word *extraversion* to refer to a complex set of attitudes and feelings tied to an orientation to the external world. Introversion was the corresponding orientation to the inner self and has been identified with introspection and thoughtfulness. However, *extraverted* has become synonymous with *sociable* and *assertive* in common use. These two conceptions of extraversion, unfortunately, are by no means equivalent. Sociable people can be introspective and loners need not be thoughtful. Guilford (1977) continues to use *extraversion* in the Jungian sense, but most other personality psychologists agree with Eysenck, popular speech, and us in defining *extra-

version as a cluster of traits marked by sociability, excitement-seeking, and assertiveness.]

The consensus on the basic dimensions of human personality probably ends with neuroticism and extraversion. But if we start from this foundation, it is relatively easy to add on new dimensions as they are needed. Suppose we found a trait that measures something of importance, but is related to neither neuroticism nor extraversion. We would want to survey the literature to see if there are other, similar traits that together might form a third dimension of personality. In our early research with the 16PF, we stumbled across such a new dimension and called it *openness to experience*. Rokeach (1960), who was interested in the structure of ideas, had written about dogmatic individuals who were not open to new ideas or values. The clinician Carl Rogers (1961) had observed that some of his clients were insensitive to their own feelings, and he proposed that openness to inner experience was a criterion of good mental health. Coan (1972) created a measure of openness to fantasy and aesthetic experience, and Tellegen and Atkinson (1974) noted that the capacity to become deeply involved in experiences, which they called *openness to absorbing experience*, was characteristic of individuals who were easily hypnotized. We see all of these traits as part of a single domain of openness. Other major dimensions (about which we will have less to say in this book) have also been proposed, including masculinity, control or conscientiousness, and agreeableness (Goldberg, 1981; Hogan, 1982).

This classification of traits might have been derived from a painstaking review of the empirical literature or even from keen observation of people. In fact, however, it has resulted chiefly from the use of a statistical technique known as *factor analysis*. The degree to which traits go together, or covary, in a group of people is first quantified; mathematical procedures are then used to identify *factors*, or dimensions, within these traits. Simply stated, factor analysis allows us to group together sets of traits that are all related to one another and unrelated to traits in other sets. If we know that a person is anxious, we can guess that he or she is hostile, since both anxiety and hostility share the dimension of neuroticism. On the other hand, knowing that someone is anxious does not tell us whether that person is warm or cold; warmth is part of extraversion and unrelated to neuroticism.

Since its development in the 1930s, factor analysis has acquired a mystique many of its proponents have been perfectly willing to preserve. The mathematical basis of the technique is beyond the sophistication of most psychologists, and theoreticians have argued at great length over which of many variations is most likely to yield correct results in a particular case. Many researchers have become embroiled in these esoteric disputes, and many others have become suspicious of the whole idea, particularly since some writers give the impression that factor analysis can magically see through the maze of poor measures, small samples, and inadequate theories to reveal the true underlying structure of personality with the same precision with which an X-ray reveals the skeleton.

From our point of view, both these extremes are unfortunate. We regard factor analysis as a very useful tool for describing the groupings of trait measures and nothing more. The more one knows about personality, from theory and from previous findings, the more intelligently one can use factor analysis. In this book we will frequently describe the results of factor analyses, but rarely dwell on the details. The basic fact established—that certain groups of measures cluster together—can be understood without any knowledge of the statistics involved.

A Three-Domain Model of Personality

When we say *personality*, we will in most cases mean individual differences in enduring dispositions. The particular dispositions we are most concerned with fall into three groups: neuroticism, extraversion, and openness to experience. We refer to this conceptualization as the NEO model (from Neuroticism, Extraversion, and Openness), and the instrument we use to measure it as the NEO Inventory. The pun on *neo-* is intentional: we regard ours as a new or perhaps reborn version of trait theory. We will have a good deal to say about the NEO model, so a few details about the traits we measure may be in order.

Eysenck (1960) has offered the simplest system of personality, consisting of two broad dimensions: extraversion and neuroticism. Appealing as this scheme is for its simplicity, it does not allow any differentiation *within* the two domains. Of two people who are equally extraverted, one may be dominant, active, and an aggressive leader who enjoys competing with others, while another may be warm, cheerful, and a cooperative follower. In some respects these two are like each other: both are strongly oriented toward interacting with other people, and both contrast sharply with the introvert who would rather be reading or working on concrete tasks, away from the crush of people. But the differences are also important. Our solution was to develop a measure of personality that contained not only global measures of the major domains, but also subscales for measuring specific facets of each.

Ideally we could claim that the six traits we identified as the facets of each domain are the basic units of personality, but there is really no justification for that statement. The facets were chosen to represent the major concepts within each domain that seem to have emerged in the past, but there is no guarantee that we have not overlooked something. Instead of being viewed as an exhaustive list, these facets should be seen as examples, representative of neuroticism, extraversion, or openness.

Is there any evidence that the traits we will discuss actually go together in the form we suggest? Indeed there is. Using factor analysis we were able to confirm the three-domain structure of traits in two samples, first in Boston and later in Baltimore (Costa and McCrae, 1980b; McCrae, 1982b). We have shown that the structure can be found in women as well as in men, in ratings as well as in self-reports, and by using different measures of the traits involved.

At one time we were intensely interested in whether the structure would be the same for old people as for young people (Costa and McCrae, 1976). We thought perhaps some reshuffling of the same basic elements might be at the basis of the age differences in personality proposed by the theories we reviewed in Chapter 1. If that had been so, this would have been a very different book; but all the evidence to date strongly suggests that the structure of personality is the same for adults of all ages.

Figure 1 (from McCrae and Costa, 1980) illustrates the NEO model with a graphic representation of the idea that traits are facets of three independent domains. A few more words about the nature of these facets is in order here.

The Eighteen NEO Facets

Anxiety and hostility, two facets of neuroticism, are the dispositional forms of two fundamental emotions: fear and anger. Everyone experiences these emotions from time to time, but the frequency and intensity with which they are felt varies from one person to another. Individuals high in the trait anxiety are nervous, high-strung, and tense. They are prone to worry; they dwell on what might go wrong. Hostile people show a similar proneness to experience anger. They tend to be irritable and ill-tempered and may prove hard to get along with.

Two different emotions, sorrow and shame, form the basis of the traits of depression and self-consciousness. As a trait, depression is the disposition to experience sadness, hopelessness, loneliness; depressed people often have feelings of guilt and of diminished self-worth. Individuals high in self-consciousness are more prone to the emotion

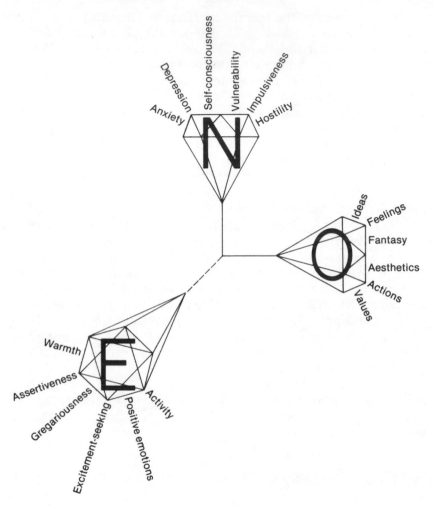

Figure 1   Schematic Representation of the Three-Dimensional, Eighteen-Facet NEO Model

of shame or embarrassment. They are particularly sensitive to ridicule and teasing, because they often feel inferior to others. (Self-consciousness is often called shyness, but it should be noted that people who are shy in this respect do not necessarily avoid people. Introverts often claim to be shy when in fact they simply do not care to interact with others and use shyness as a good excuse.)

Two of the facets of neuroticism are more often manifest in behaviors than in emotional states. Impulsiveness is the tendency to give in to temptations and to be overwhelmed by desires. Because they have so little control (or perhaps because they experience such strong urges), impulsive people tend to overeat and overspend, to drink and smoke, gamble, and perhaps use drugs. Vulnerability designates an inability to deal adequately with stress. Vulnerable people tend to panic in emergencies, to break down, and to become dependent on others for help.

Some individuals will be anxious but not hostile, or self-conscious but not impulsive. But in general, those high in neuroticism are likely to be high in *each* of these traits. They are prone to violent and negative emotions that interfere with their ability to deal with their problems and to get along with others. We can envision the kind of chain of events such a person may experience: in social situations he is anxious and embarrassed, and his frustration in dealing with others may make him hostile, further complicating matters. In compensation he turns to the use of alcohol or food, and the long-term results are likely to be depressing. Although the emotions and impulses that disturb him may not occur simultaneously, they succeed one another with distressing regularity.

The facets of extraversion can be subdivided into three interpersonal and three temperamental traits. Warmth, or attachment, refers to a friendly, compassionate, intimately involved style of personal interaction; by contrast, cold individuals are more likely to be formal and impersonal, with weak attachments to most other people. Warmth and gregariousness (the desire to be with other people) together make up what is sometimes called sociability. Gregarious people like crowds; they seem to relish sheer quantity of social stimulation. Assertive people are natural leaders, easily taking charge, making up their own minds, and readily expressing their feelings and desires.

The three forms of extraversion we have called temperamental are activity, excitement-seeking, and positive emotions. Extraverts like to keep busy, acting vigorously and talking rapidly; they are energetic and forceful. They also prefer environments that stimulate them, often going in search of excitement. Fast cars, flashy clothes, risky undertakings hold an attraction for them. The active and exciting life of extraverts is reflected emotionally in the experience of positive emotions. Joy, delight, zest, and jocularity are part of the package of traits in the domain of extraversion. Once again, all these dispositions are synergistic, working together to form a personality syndrome. Activity leads to excitement and excitement to happiness; the happy person finds others easier to get along with, and congeniality easily turns to leadership.

We measure openness to experience in six different areas. In fantasy openness implies a vivid imagination and a tendency to develop elaborate daydreams; in aesthetics it is seen in sensitivity to art and beauty. Aesthetic experience is perhaps the epitome of openness, since it is pure experience for its own sake; we know from studies of occupational interests that a preference for artistic activities is especially characteristic of open people. As Rogers might have predicted, open individuals experience their own feelings strongly, and they value the experience, seeing it as a source of meaning in life.

Openness to action is the opposite of rigidity; open people are willing to try a new dish or see a new movie or travel to a foreign country. Openness to ideas and values is also part of the domain; open people are curious and value knowledge for its own sake. Perhaps because they are willing to think of different possibilities and to empathize with others in other circumstances, they tend to be liberal in values, admitting that what is right and wrong for one person may not be applicable in other circumstances.

Making Distinctions

It is not difficult to see the relations between traits within a single domain. But it can be difficult to make the distinctions between domains that the facts demand. Human beings have a tendency to evaluate ideas and organize them in terms of good and bad. It is easy to see neuroticism as bad and extraversion and openness as good, and then to assume that individuals high in neuroticism are likely to be introverted and closed to experience. It doesn't work that way. The three domains are independent; consequently, an individual high in neuroticism is as likely to be extraverted as introverted and as likely to be open as closed. Three dimensions cannot be collapsed into one without serious distortions.

One way to make the necessary conceptual distinctions is to concentrate on the opposite poles, the low ends, of the traits we are discussing. Introverts are cold, but not hostile; loners, but not self-conscious; not particularly cheerful, but not necessarily depressed either. Individuals who are closed to experience are not necessarily maladjusted; in fact, they are somewhat less likely to experience violent emotions by virtue of their lesser sensitivity to emotions of all kinds. They may not care to travel to strange places and meet unusual people, but they are just as likely as open people to seek excitement and crowds of people—as long as both are of the familiar variety.

There is another mistake in contrasting "good" and "bad" dimensions of personality: we may be mistaken about which is which. From the individual's point of view, there are distinct advantages to being well-adjusted and extraverted. Well-adjusted, extraverted people usually report themselves to be the happiest, the most satisfied with life (Costa and McCrae, 1980a). But from society's point of view, all kinds of people are necessary: those who work well with others and those who can finish a task on their own, those who come up with creative new ways of doing things and those who maintain the best solutions of the past. There are probably even advantages to be found in neuroticism, since a society of extremely easygoing individuals might not compete well with other societies of suspicious and hostile individuals. Some theorists (Hogan, 1979) have even suggested that such societal advantages may account for individual differences in an evolutionary sense: human beings have evolved consistent differences because this range of characteristics is useful in the survival of the social group.

From Concepts to Data:
Measuring Personality

The whole trick of science is to test ideas against reality, and in order to do that, we must measure something. We may suspect that salespeople are likely to be extraverts, but in order to prove it we have to be able to measure extraversion and to convince other people that we are measuring it successfully. If we can come that far, it is a relatively easy matter to see whether salespeople score higher than others on our measure, although we also have to be concerned with the representativeness of our sample of salespeople, the magnitude of the difference we find, and any number of other problems in interpretation.

In many respects, trait theories of personality are among the easiest to operationalize (as the process of finding suitable measures for theoretical concepts is called). Traits are generalized dispositions, so we know we must look for evidence of consistent patterns of behavior or reactions across a range of situations. Traits endure over time, so we know that our measures must give us about the same results when applied at two different times, say a few weeks apart. Individuals vary in the degree to which they can be characterized by a trait, so we may want to look at the frequency and intensity of responses.

Based on the description of extraversion in the NEO model, we might be able to measure extraversion by getting the answers to the following questions:

How many close friends does this person have?
How much does this person enjoy parties?
Is this person often leader of the group?
How active and energetic is this person?
How much does this person crave excitement?
Is this person usually cheerful?

If we come up with a reasonable system for answering all these questions, say on a scale from 1 to 5, we can add up the numbers and assign a score for extraversion. Once we have the answers for a sample of people, we can check the serviceability of our measure by asking some simple questions. First, do these items generally agree in the picture they give of the individual? That is, do people with many close friends also tend to be energetic and cheerful? (This is technically called *internal consistency*, and it provides evidence that the different behaviors or reactions are actually part of a pattern and not just a collection of unrelated activities.) If not, either we have a bad set of questions or we have misunderstood the nature of extraversion. Second, do the scores people get on one occasion parallel the scores they get at a later time? Are the extraverts of January still extraverts in March? (This is called *retest reliability* and demonstrates that what is being measured is a trait, not a temporary state or mood of the individual.)

There is little dispute about any of this. Most psychologists agree on what kinds of answers we need; the problem comes in deciding how we should get the answers. How do we know how much a person enjoys parties? We could ask the person, but she may never have thought about it or may lie to us or may unconsciously distort the answer. We could ask friends, but they may not know how the person really feels and may have seen only one side of her personality. We could watch the person at a party and note how much she smiles, how long she stays, how excited she seems to be, but her behavior at this party may be atypical. Perhaps she has a toothache, or perhaps she does not get along with the host.

Behaviorally oriented psychologists would prefer the third strategy, since it seems to be the most objective and scientific. But as we have pointed out, the contributions of dispositions to observable behavior are often overshadowed by the press of circumstances, and recent studies have shown that behavior has to be observed over many occasions before reliable inferences can be made about traits (Epstein, 1979). In principle, repeated observation is perfectly reasonable; in practice, it is prohibitively expensive and time-consuming.

Furthermore, observations of behavior, regardless of their number, may not be the most accurate source of answers. If we are really interested in the individual's dispositions, how the person feels may be much more relevant than how she acts. It may be necessary to put on a front, to play a role, to seem instead of being. A simple question asked in a way that allows for candid answers may produce a far truer picture of real dispositions. In some areas, such as happiness, it can reasonably be argued that personal opinion is the *only* meaningful criterion.

It would hardly be an exaggeration to say that trait psychology has been floundering over these issues for the past thirty years. The great majority of researchers have been content to hand out questionnaires and trust the self-reports of their subjects, but their conclusions have been dismissed time and again because of objections about the kinds of errors to which self-report instruments are prone (Edwards, 1957; Block, 1965). Behaviorists have scoffed at the idea that paper-and-pencil measures can be a substitute for the observations of real behavior. Psychodynamic theorists have objected that unconscious defense mechanisms or more or less conscious tendencies to present a socially desirable face make self-reports suspect. Social psychologists have contended that what counts is the perception of behavior by significant others and that in consequence only ratings should be trusted.

At last, however, there is some prospect that these controversies will be resolved. We know only too well that any method of measurement, any source of answers to our questions, is subject to certain kinds of error and that consequently the surest results are those which can be seen using several different methods. But we are also beginning to see convincing evidence that, properly employed, many methods can give a reasonable approximation to the truth. A growing body of studies has shown that different methods do lead to the same conclusions about people.

One line of research has been concerned with correspondence between objective, observable behavior and self-reports. In one study (McGowan and Gormly, 1976), researchers followed a small group of college students and clocked their speed of walking. The fastest walkers were the ones who reported the highest activity level and who were rated by their peers as most energetic—not a particularly exciting result for the average reader, but a revelation for those psychologists who thought that self-reports were totally untrustworthy. Similarly, Small, Zeldin, and Savin-Williams (1983) recorded altruistic and dominant behaviors of small groups of teenagers on a summer camping trip and also asked the campers to rate each other on these two dimensions. They found remarkably high agreement between their behavior counts and the peer perceptions. Another version of this line of research (Epstein, 1977) has demonstrated that as the sample of behavior increases, the correspondence between observations and self-reports increases to quite respectable levels.

A different tack has been taken sporadically over the past thirty years in comparisons of self-reports and ratings. Rate yourself on the six questions listed earlier on a 1-to-5 scale, and then ask a friend who knows you well to rate you. You may be surprised at the differences of opinion. We would be guilty of failing to learn from a decade of criticism if we did not acknowledge that there is a substantial element of illusion in the views we hold of others (Fiske, 1978) and in our idea of their views of us (Swann, in press). We easily and rapidly form opinions about others' personalities, often with little basis in fact. This is particularly true of those with whom we have only a passing acquaintance.

But as we live and work with others over a period of months or years, repeated observations lead us to correct our impressions of them, and lead us to a better understanding of us. Enough studies have now been done to assert that ratings from qualified raters agree substantially with self-reports (McCrae, 1982b). We also think we know that some traits (like anxiety) are more easily rated than others (like self-consciousness), that long-term acquaintances are better raters than are short-term acquaintances, and that average ratings from a group of people are generally better than ratings from a single source. There are still a number of unresolved issues here (for example, who should be believed if rater and self-reporter sharply disagree?), but the general conclusion is that both self-reports and ratings provide reasonable approximations to the truth.

*   *   *

The meaningfulness of trait psychology and the validity of self-report measures of traits are crucial to all the other arguments about aging and personality we will offer. All the data reviewed in Chapter 2 were based on self-reports of traits, and what they showed was neither more nor less than that older people do not differ from younger people in the average level of self-reported personality traits. In Chapter 5 we will return to theories of personality and see if other conceptualizations of personality with other forms of measurement lead to different conclusions.

In the meantime we will assume that we have provided adequate justification for looking seriously at what happens to traits over the course of an individual's life. We have argued that traits are indispensable both for laypeople and for psychological theorists; that there is growing agreement about how many important groups of traits there are and which characteristics they include; and that there is increasing evidence that several measurement techniques lead to the same basic conclusions and thus are dependable bases for inferences about aging and personality. Lastly, it seems to us that the disparagement of traits as trivial aspects of personality is ill-founded. Anxiety, warmth, and intellectual curiosity are extremely important characteristics of individuals, especially if they persist across the life span. In the next chapter we will review the evidence on the constancy of individual characteristics.

Chapter

4

The Course
of Personality
in the Individual

We have used the word *stability* repeatedly with the assumption that its meaning is obvious. But in fact, stability has several meanings, and a discussion of them is a necessary prologue to a fuller look at the data on personality and aging. Different kinds of statistical tests and sometimes different methods of collecting data are necessary when one is looking for different types of stability and change. Some kinds of stability are frankly uninteresting; others form the basis for a whole new way of thinking about the course of human lives.

Two Different Questions: Stability and Change
in Groups and in Individuals

In Chapter 2 we reviewed at some length the evidence on stability of mean levels of personality traits. In the simplest case, the cross-sectional study, we found that old people generally scored neither higher nor lower than young people on a variety of personality measures—for example, anxiety. (Several longitudinal studies concurred in finding no changes in the average level of anxiety.) This failure to find change in personality contrasts with the evidence of age-related changes in a number of functions. In childhood, for example, intelligence, vocabulary, and physical size and strength obviously increase through adolescence. In later adulthood, declines in strength, memory, and hearing are equally well documented. Anxiety, on the other hand, does not show a pattern of rising or falling as people age.

In all these examples, whether of change or stability, we are comparing the average levels of groups of individuals. There are good reasons for concentrating on the average or mean level of a trait when we are interested in the effects of age. We know that most traits show a wide distribution, with some individuals high, some low, and many intermediate in the degree to which they manifest the trait. We can rarely make assertions of the form "All eighty-year-olds are higher in X than all seventy-year-olds." If a psychologist is careless enough to say that old people have poor memories, he is sure to hear dozens of stories about old people with good memories or young people with worse ones. When so pressed, he is likely to rephrase the statement to say that *on the average* old people have poorer memories. "Of course," he might continue, "some people have better memories, some worse; they may have been born that way, or they may have developed skills through practice or education. Medications or illnesses or psychological states may interfere with memory performance. But I'm not interested in any of those things. I'm interested in the effects of age on memory. So my strategy is to measure a large group of people, some old, some young. Some of the old ones will be naturally bright, some naturally not so bright; some will be well-educated, some poorly educated. When I look at the group average, all those differences will cancel each other out. The only thing all these people have in common, and thus the only thing that will be characteristic of the group average, is the fact that they are older. The same logic applies to the young group. When I compare the average older subject with the average younger subject, any differences must be due to age."

In Chapter 2 we questioned the assumption that the only respect in which two such groups differed systematically was age, pointing out that they might well also differ in average education, health status, or other features. But if we can assume that those other characteristics have been controlled through a careful selection of subjects, the logic of cross-sectional comparisons is sound. Individual differences in memory are attributable either to age or to some other factors. The interest in studies of this sort is always in the first source of individual differences; other differences are something of a nuisance, a source of possible confusion. In statistical models, they contribute to what is called an *error term*. If everyone started out with exactly the same capacity for memory, it would be much easier to see the effects of age. But people do not start off with the same abilities, just as they do not start off with the same levels of anxiety or assertiveness or openness to ideas. In early adulthood we find wide variation in all the personality traits of interest to us. We find the same range of differences among old people. We know from the studies in Chapter 2 that people as a whole or on the average do not change much during adulthood; but so far we have said very little about what *individuals* do.

Ms. Smith may be docile and traditional as a newlywed, but thirty years later she may have become assertive and unconventional. Mr. Jones may be interested in automotive mechanics and sports during his twenties, but be devoted to Bible readings by the time he is sixty. Then again, Ms. Smith may still be docile and traditional and Mr. Jones still interested in sports when both are past seventy.

This is a question of stability or change not of a group of people, but of individuals. The study of changes in individuals is considerably more complicated and correspondingly more interesting than the study of changes in groups. If the group as a whole changes, we can be sure that at least some of the individuals have changed, but the converse is not necessarily true. The average level of the group may not be altered even though *all* the individuals change—if, for example, there are as many who increase as decrease. Finding out that groups are stable, then, does not rule out the possibility that individuals change; and, in fact, a number of fascinating possibilities for individual development are consistent with the findings of group stability.

There is a major methodological difference between the study of groups and the study of individuals. To make inferences about mean changes with age, we need only compare groups of different ages (provided we can be relatively sure they do not differ in any other characteristics). Any two groups of people will do, so the cross-sectional design is a convenient, if not foolproof, method of obtaining a quick answer. We need not wait for the passage of time.

But a study of individual changes requires that we examine the same person at two or more ages; longitudinal studies with repeated measurements of the same subjects are essential. As a result, the data available on which to base conclusions are much slimmer and of much more recent vintage. Only in the past decade have more than a handful of studies been published in which longitudinal data on personality were reported. Fortunately, all these studies have been in substantial agreement, and so we can draw our conclusions with considerable confidence.

There is, however, one approach in this area that parallels the cross-sectional study as a quick method of seeing what changes occur to an individual over the life span. In the retrospective study, people are asked to recall what they were like at earlier ages and to compare their present state. On the whole, psychologists have been extremely leery of this kind of research. Memory, they maintain, has ways of playing tricks on people. In fact, a number of studies have shown that people can and do distort the past, whether consciously or not. Many more people, for example, "remember" voting for the winning candidate than the election results could possibly allow. With one exception (to be discussed later), there has been virtually no research comparing memories of earlier personality with actual records. However, the recent harvest of longitudinal findings allows us to compare retrospective reports with objective facts. As we will see, they suggest that conclusions based on life histories generally square with prospective longitudinal findings.

Developmental Patterns in Individuals

Although most personality theorists assume that adult personality is in some way an outgrowth or developmental continuation of earlier personality, other views are also possible. Some writers (Schweder, 1975) wholly deny the reality of personality, assigning to it the status of a myth or a metaphysical existence like that of the soul. So elusive and insubstantial an entity could hardly be said either to change or to stay the same, and the whole issue is banished from the realm of scientific inquiry. A more moderate position might hold that personality is like mood—a real enough phenomenon, but one that comes and goes according to laws so obscure that it seems completely random. Finally, a number of contemporary psychologists would probably conceptualize personality as largely a function of the immediate or at least recent environment. They might see extraversion, for example, as a set of learned responses to social situations. One's environment may change radically as one goes from parents' home to college to one work situation and then another and finally to a retirement home. In some of these situations the person may be rewarded for friendliness, leadership, and energetic behavior. In others, independence, compliance, or quiet may be preferred and reinforced. After months or years in such circumstances, the individual may come to internalize the system of rewards and punishments, to assume the qualities promoted by the environment. His personality may change.

Note that this kind of change is not necessarily age-related. Chance (Bandura, 1982) may play a large role. What are neighbors like? What jobs are available? What does the family expect, and what are the effects of remarriage or of having or losing children? Conceivably one might be an introvert at twenty, forty, and sixty and an extravert at thirty, fifty, and seventy. Later personality might not be predictable at all from earlier personality. If there were any continuity in personality, it could be attributed to the stability of supporting environments. If the life structure remains the same, personality will too; but a change in the one should lead to a change in the other.

This position, compatible with some versions of social learning theory, is appealing to neither personality theorists nor developmentalists. It locates the origin of behavior in the external circumstances, temporarily internalized, but easily replaced when circumstances change. Personologists like to believe that personality is an intrinsic part of the person, changeable perhaps, but not quite so readily and with so little regard for the qualities that the individual brings to her exchanges with the environment. Developmentalists would also take exception to this view, since they see personality as something that unfolds more or less naturally, each phase an outgrowth of earlier developments. Personality is something with a history, they would say, not simply a mirror of current events.

Of course, the fact that the social learning view of personality is distasteful to those interested in personality and aging does not in the least mean that it is wrong. Ten years ago, in fact, a majority of psychologists would probably have said that it was correct (many still would). At that time there were few studies that could really address the issue, but a number have since appeared.

True or false, the social learning view is certainly less beguiling than developmental theories, with their sometimes elaborate chains of growth, unfolding, and transformation. Central to the idea of development is the notion of *continuity*: in any developmental sequence, a single organism goes through a series of changes, each an expression of the same underlying entity. The butterfly is the natural outgrowth of the caterpillar, as different as the two are in form and function. The environment may hasten or retard, facilitate or damage the transformation, but caterpillars will never turn into spiders, no matter what environments we impose on them. The same basic genetic material endures through and is manifest in successive stages of development.

Most of the theorizing about the course of personality in the individual has been offered by child developmentalists (Block and Block, 1980; Kagan and Moss, 1962; Thomas, Chess, and Birch, 1968) interested in accounting for personality from the period of infancy through adolescence, although a few theorists have carried the idea through adulthood. The attempt to account for the origins of personality in childhood is immensely attractive, since childhood seems to be the time when the most could be done to change or improve lifelong patterns of adjustment. At the same time, it is an extraordinarily ambitious undertaking. It is easy enough to chart the course of extraversion, say, in an adult: simply have him or her fill out a questionnaire every ten years or so. But we cannot ask a five-year-old to complete a questionnaire; we cannot ask an infant even a few simple questions. How, then, do we measure personality—by observations of behavior? What kind of infant behavior corresponds to openness to aesthetic experience? Is it even meaningful to ask about this dimension of personality before adolescence?

Fortunately, we do not need to solve these problems here. Other writers, more knowledgeable in the area, have struggled with them and offered their own answers. The issue concerns us here, however, because the same answers may be useful in conceptualizing the course of personality in adulthood.

One of the more elaborate models has been labeled *heterotypic* [or *different-form*] *continuity* (Kagan, 1971). Just as an insect goes through four distinct but developmentally related stages, so too may personality evolve through a succession of distinct phases. Sociability in adulthood may be the consequence not of sociability in childhood, but of some very different trait—say, academic interests. If we watched an unsociable but intellectual child develop into a warm and friendly adult, we might believe that we had seen a failure of continuity. But if we watched a whole group of intellectual children become sociable adults, we would believe we had discovered a pattern, a kind of dispositional metamorphosis. (We might then attempt to explain the transformation: perhaps the social advantages of a good education lead to a more congenial environment in adulthood, making the person more friendly. Or perhaps both academic pursuits in childhood and sociability in adulthood reflect an underlying tendency to please significant others in one's life. Speculations on what might account for such relationships are endless and endlessly intriguing, which may account for the popularity of this model with many developmentalists.) Almost any trait in childhood may develop into almost any other; and of course the changes need not be limited to childhood. Young adults may develop into older adults with quite different, but quite predictable, sets of traits (Livson, 1973).

For a time (before additional data disillusioned us) we thought we had found just such a pattern (Costa and McCrae, 1976). In looking at cross-sectional data on several aspects of openness to experience, we seemed to see a shift in the aspects of experience to which open men were open. In young men, when youthful romanticism was at its peak, openness was expressed as a sensitivity to feelings and to aesthetic experiences. In middle age, when the responsibilities of raising a family and furthering a career were uppermost, the same openness was seen in a more intellectual form, of which curiosity and a willingness to reformulate traditional values were the hallmarks. Finally, in the wisdom of old age, the open person was sensitized to both feelings and thoughts, both beauty and truth. Since differentiation and subsequent integration are familiar developmental processes (Werner, 1957), this sequence seemed to provide a classic case of personality development in adulthood.

We had to abandon this model soon after we proposed it, because we found that later and better data offered no support for it whatsoever. Individuals who are open to feelings and aesthetic experiences tend also to be open to ideas and values (and actions and fantasy) at *all* ages in adulthood. This is as true for women as for men, our later studies showed (McCrae, 1982b). Age, it now appears, has nothing to do with it.

But it is easy to see why this model would appeal to developmentalists. Sequences of heterotypic continuity make fascinating stories. They are also far from obvious and thus allow the investigator to seemingly discover a pattern in nature that has eluded the grasp of naive observation. Finally, such sequences are elusive and thus give to developmentalists who have been unable to find the kind of regular change they seek a reason to hope that continued observation may yet pay off.

This model has most frequently been discussed by researchers interested in personality development in early childhood, when observable behavior (such as the smiles or cries of an infant) may bear only the vaguest resemblance to later personality traits like sociability or anxiety. Its use there may or may not be justified—a good deal more research is needed before we will know for sure.

One version, however, is familiar to students of adult personality development. As we noted in Chapter 1, Jung (1923) proposed one of the first models of adult personality development as part of his vast and intricate psychology of personality. Instead of traits, he described various functions or structures in the psyche that governed the flow of behavior and experience. The anima and animus, for example, are parts of the self corresponding to the feminine part of the man, the masculine part of the woman. Thought and feeling, sensation and intuition are functions of the mind for perceiving and evaluating reality. The persona is the part of our personality we show to others; the shadow, the part we conceal. All these and more form the self, and the goal of adult life is the full development and expression—the individuation—of the self.

For Jung, most of these functions and structures are opposites and cannot operate simultaneously. We cannot at once be masculine and feminine, intuitive and logical, courteous and contemptuous. If all these are to be expressed, they will have to take turns. Jung proposed that this balancing process would take a lifetime; he hypothesized that the functions which dominated youth would be replaced by their opposites in old age. The aggressive, forceful young man would become docile and passive with age; the passive young woman would become aggressive. Gutmann (1970), you may recall, proposed this particular transformation as a general rule.

It is somewhat hazardous to suppose that the functions hypothesized by Jung correspond to anything as straightforward as traits, but the notion of balancing might easily be applied to them. Instead of supposing, as the heterotypic continuity model does, that any trait may give rise to any other trait, we might suppose that each trait will lead into its own opposite. We can then predict what an individual's personality will be like in old age by reversing the characteristics seen in youth. Neurotic will be adjusted, introvert will be extravert, open will be closed.

Finally, there is one more model, one more possible developmental sequence: there may be no change at all. Depressed youth may become depressed elderly; talkative oldsters may once have been talkative youngsters. It may seem strange to speak of development when there is no change, so perhaps this should be distinguished as a personological rather than a developmental model. But it shares with developmental schemes the central notion of continuity. Personality, according to this theory, is not at the mercy of the immediate environment; indeed, it withstands all the shocks of life and of aging. Catastrophic events—illnesses, wars, great losses—may alter personality, as may effective therapeutic intervention. But according to stability theory, the natural course of personality in adulthood is unchanging.

Investigating the Course of Personality Traits

Cross-sectional studies of personality traits tell us nothing at all about their natural histories. For that, we must trace them through the lives of aging individuals. If we are interested in formulating general principles and not simply writing individual biographies, we have to have data from reasonably large samples of individuals. And if we have enough information to draw valid conclusions, we probably have too much to be able to understand it by simply inspecting it with the unaided mind. We have to resort to statistical summaries of the data, and of these the most important for the present purpose is the correlation coefficient.

A *correlation* is a mutual relation between two things, a tendency for one to vary as the other does. A *correlation coefficient* is a measure of the degree of correlation of two variables, ranging from −1.0 to +1.0. Positive correlations indicate that the second variable increases as the first increases; negative correlations mean that the second increases as the first decreases. A correlation of 0.0 signifies independence, or a complete absence of association between variables. The greater the departure from zero, the stronger the association. For peculiar statistical reasons, the most meaningful expression of the strength of the relationship is usually given by the square of the correlation. Thus, if two tests have a correlation of .80, we know that the higher one scores on the first, the higher one is likely to score on the other, and that about 64 percent (or .80 squared) of the information in the second test is predictable from the first test.

We have gone into this technical point because the correlation coefficient is virtually indispensable to a discussion of traits. We have already mentioned several of its uses. The internal consistency of trait measures and their retest reliability are assessed by forms of the correlation coefficient. Factor analysis uses correlation coefficients to group traits into broader domains. The degree of agreement between self-reports and observer ratings of personality traits is expressed as a correlation. An alternative to the comparison of young and old group averages in a cross-sectional study is the correlation of the trait with age (in the area of personality, these latter correlations are, of course, near zero).

The correlation coefficient is so useful because it is a standard of comparison that is independent of the nature of the variables being correlated. Correlations between height and weight, IQ and grades, hostility and anxiety can all be expressed by the same number. Any two variables that can be measured on the same subjects can be correlated, although normally the correlation is near zero when quite different things (like shoe size and liberalism) are compared.

The price one pays for that universal metric is a certain amount of ambiguity. We cannot, for example, tell which of two variables (if either) is the cause and which the effect: the correlation between A and B is exactly the same as the correlation between B and A. As we will see shortly, we cannot tell anything about the average level of the variables. And although the measure is completely standardized and exactly understood in a mathematical sense, it can be very difficult to interpret conceptually.

What, for example, is a high or good or impressive or strong correlation? What is moderate? What is modest or weak? These disarmingly simple questions are the source of profound controversy in psychology. Being human, researchers tend to consider the correlations that support their point of view strong and the correlations that support other positions weak. Even the most unbiased judgment, however, must somehow take into account a range of considerations, including the expected magnitude of association, the size of correlations typically found in that field of research, the relative size of other correlations, and the reliability of the measuring instruments.

In a few cases standards have become generally accepted. Reliability coefficients for personality tests, for example, are supposed to be in the vicinity of .70 to .90; most researchers would look askance at a test whose internal consistency was .40. In the prediction of behavior from a personality test, on the other hand, .40 would be quite respectable. One statistician, Jacob Cohen (1969), offered his expectations for psychological research in a set of rules of thumb: .10 is weak, .30 is moderate, and .50 or better is a strong correlation. It may be useful to the reader to consider a few familiar examples. The correlation of aptitude tests with college grades is about .40 to .60 (Edwards, 1954); height and weight show a correlation of roughly .70 (Peatman, 1947); and self-reports of anxiety and depression correlate about .60 in the BLSA.

If we obtained a set of measurements of personality traits and several years later measured the same set of people once more on the same set of traits, we would have the minimum information necessary to begin to evaluate the alternative theoretical positions we have described above. We would need to determine the correlation of each trait at the first time with each trait at the second. We could then make quite specific hypotheses about what we expected to find.

If the social learning position is correct in positing that personality is freely reshaped by changing circumstances, there should be little or no correlation between any of the traits at the first time and any of the traits at the second. If sufficient time has elapsed to allow many individuals in the sample to move, change jobs, marry, or have children, we should expect substantial change in personality for many people in unpredictable directions. Thus, personality at time 2 should be unrelated to personality at time 1. We might expect modest correlations (say .30) between corresponding traits at the two times because some individuals would have remained in the same environments, which might have sustained the traits.

The heterotypic continuity model would predict high correlations somewhere, but it might not be possible to predict just where they would occur. Extraversion at time 1 might be strongly correlated at time 2 with openness or with closedness or with neuroticism. The distinctive feature of this model is that we would *not* expect extraversion at time 1 to be correlated chiefly with extraversion at time 2. It is principally for this reason that we would not want to conduct a study in which *only* extraversion was measured at two times: if the heterotypic continuity model is correct, we would miss important evidence of personality continuity and transformation because we would not have assessed the trait into which extraversion metamorphosed.

The balancing model of personality development is somewhat easier to evaluate, because we know the direction of the change we are supposed to expect. If we measure traits at the beginning of adulthood and then again at the end, we would expect a strong correlation between corresponding measurements of each trait—but we would hypothesize that the correlation would be *negative*. The extreme introvert would have become the extreme extravert, the feminine person would have become masculine, the open individual would have become closed. The predictions of this model, however, are somewhat harder to anticipate if the time span between measurements is a matter of years instead of decades, since individuals may not yet have reached a point of crossover. We would, however, expect great variability among individuals at the beginning and end of adulthood, but similarity among the middle-aged, all of whom are nearing the central crossover point.

Finally, the predictions of the stability model are straightforward: if personality traits are relatively unchanging over the years, there should be high positive correlations between corresponding traits over the two times; and the correlations of each trait with itself over time should be higher than the correlations across time between different traits. In other words, the same pattern that we call re-test reliability when a test is readministered after a month would be seen as stability of personality if it were readministered after a decade.

Longitudinal Evidence

Many of the studies we described in Chapter 2 as sources of longitudinal evidence about changes in the average levels of traits have also provided evidence about the course of traits in individuals. However, a number of other studies have also contributed to this body of evidence. As an example, we examine the data from the Baltimore Longitudinal Study of Aging for the 114 men who took the Guilford-Zimmerman Temperament Survey (GZTS) on three occasions about six years apart (Costa, McCrae, and Arenberg, 1980). Table 1 gives the observed intercorrelations among the ten traits across twelve years from the first to the third administration.

Several things are immediately apparent from an examination of this table. Most obvious are the correlations, shown in boldface, that indicate the stability of individual traits. These correlations, ranging from .68 to .85, are extraordinarily high. Psychologists might expect to see correlations this high if the measures were administered twelve days apart, but not twelve years; and in fact, the stability coefficients presented here are somewhat higher than the short-term reliabilities reported in the test manual (Guilford, Zimmerman, and Guilford, 1976). Given that mean levels change very little (as we saw in Chapter 2), it becomes clear that most individuals obtain almost exactly the same scores on these tests on two different occasions separated by twelve years.

If these data were the only evidence of this exceptional degree of

Table 1
Correlations among 10 Personality Traits over 12 Years

Third administration	First administration									
	1	2	3	4	5	6	7	8	9	10
1 General activity	80	-13	38	27	22	21	-15	-01	-03	-09
2 Restraint	-13	71	-21	-33	-03	-05	13	18	01	04
3 Ascendance	38	-19	85	58	33	29	-13	16	10	04
4 Sociability	29	-33	54	75	21	28	-01	-06	04	-13
5 Emotional stability	15	-02	39	35	71	66	35	-20	37	13
6 Objectivity	06	-02	30	30	51	74	48	-16	37	24
7 Friendliness	-24	15	-23	-04	27	41	77	-21	35	18
8 Thoughtfulness	11	16	11	-03	-16	18	-28	71	-29	-09
9 Personal relations	-12	-05	07	05	13	25	23	-13	68	34
10 Masculinity	-03	-07	11	-04	19	32	17	-12	24	73

Note: Correlations > .24 significant at $p < .01$. $N = 114$. Decimal points omitted.

stability in personality, we would quite properly be skeptical; but a number of other studies have reported similar findings. In the Boston study we found ten-year stability coefficients of .69 for neuroticism and .84 for extraversion (Costa and McCrae, 1977). Researchers at Duke University (Siegler, George, and Okun, 1979) found correlations of about .50 for eight-year intervals, using a test with somewhat lower reliability to begin with. Leon and her colleagues (1979) reported stability coefficients ranging from .28 to .74 using the MMPI (a widely used measure of psychopathology) for a sample of seventy-one men measured at middle age and then again thirty years later. As long ago as 1955, Strong showed that occupational interests (which are closely related to personality dispositions) were highly stable after the age of twenty-five. In short, a substantial body of literature unanimously shows that individuals change very little in self-reported personality traits over periods of up to thirty years and over the age range from twenty to ninety.

Consider what that means. In the course of thirty years, many individuals will have undergone radical changes in their life structures. They may have married, divorced, remarried. They have probably moved their residence several times. Job changes, layoffs, promotions, and retirement are all likely to have occurred for many people. Close friends and confidants will have died or moved away or become alienated. Children will have been born, grown up, married, begun a family of their own. The individual will have aged biologically, with changes in appearance, health, vigor, memory, and sensory abilities. Internationally, wars, depressions, and social movements will have come and gone. Most subjects will have read dozens of books, seen hundreds of movies, watched thousands of hours of television. *And yet, most people will not have changed appreciably in any of the personality dispositions measured by these tests.*

The idea that personality should be so deeply and permanently ingrained is revolutionary in a scientific climate in which change, growth, and development are the watchwords. Not surprisingly, therefore, a number of psychologists have challenged the basic findings. We will return shortly to a discussion of their arguments and our replies; but first it would be useful to take a second look at Table 1 to see what it suggests about the alternative models of personality continuity.

We need only consider the continuity models, because the data seem sharply inconsistent with any positions that do not recognize the continuity of personality. It is hardly believable to suggest that external environments have remained unchanged over intervals of up to thirty years—that would be far more puzzling than the stability of personality. And within the continuity models, the choice seems equally clear. The Jungian notion of balancing would predict *negative* correlations for the retest of traits over long intervals; our correlations are strongly *positive*.

The heterotypic continuity model also fails to account for the results in Table 1. True, there are some sizeable correlations between traits at the first administration and different traits at the third. Ascendance, for example, predicts later sociability with an impressive correlation of .54. But before concluding that ascendance *develops into* sociability, we should note that the reverse is equally true: sociability predicts ascendance twelve years later with a correlation of .58. Finally (though it is not shown on Table 1), the correlation of ascendance with sociability when both are measured at the same time is .64 at the first administration and .58 at the third administration. In short, regardless of when either is measured, the correlation of these two traits is about .6, a fact which is not in the least surprising when one recalls that both are facets of the domain of extraversion. In the same way, strong predictive correlations are found between different traits in the domain of neuroticism, such as emotional stability and objectivity. But none of the heterotypic correlations are as strong as the correlation of each trait with itself over time; and none of the predictive correlations cross the boundaries of their own domains. Extraversion does not predict neuroticism; masculinity does not predict restraint.

Methodological Issues in the Assessment of Stability

When unexpected—or unwanted—results are found, there is a strong tendency to dismiss them. This reluctance to accept an unforeseen result is not really a result of closedmindedness, nor is it unscientific. On the contrary, the essence of science is to look critically at observations and conclusions. Every scientist knows that there is more than one explanation for any phenomenon and is rightfully wary of accepting the first account that offers itself. True, the high correlations between personality scores at two different times are just what one would expect if personality is actually highly stable. But there are a number of other explanations of the same correlations which are entirely consistent with major change in personality. Until these rival hypotheses can be ruled out, it is premature to accept the conclusion of stability.

The first and most fundamental challenge to any interpretation of data is the notion of chance: perhaps the correlations are a fluke. In this particular case that argument is extremely weak. Statistically, the likelihood of observing correlations of this size in samples this large purely by chance is less than one in 10,000. And it would be coincidence indeed if we happened to exceed these odds not only for activity, but also for restraint, ascendance, sociability, and so on. No scientist would seriously suggest that these are chance results.

One might argue, however, that the results are not generalizable. Perhaps we observe such high stability only because of the sample we use. Women were not included in this data set; blacks and other nonwhites were greatly underrepresented; education, social class, and intelligence were markedly higher in the BLSA study than they are in the full population. Perhaps these characteristics somehow explain the observed stability. But our conclusions are not based on the Baltimore study alone. We have also seen similar evidence from research at Duke and Minnesota, as well as our own earlier work in Boston. Thus, there is strong replicability of results over samples that are considerably more diverse and representative than the BLSA.

The same argument—and the same answer—applies to considerations of measures. If stability were found only when the Guilford-Zimmerman Temperament Survey was used, we would begin to suspect that GZTS scores, not personality dispositions, were stable, and we would then try to determine what peculiarity about the GZTS accounted for its constancy. But highly similar results have been seen with the MMPI and the 16PF; in fact, every personality inventory that has been longitudinally examined has shown exceptional levels of stability.

And so the attack shifts ground. If it is not a specific personality test that accounts for stability, perhaps it is the nature of personality tests themselves. All of the tests we have reviewed are self-report inventories, in which we base our assessment of the individual on the ways in which he or she responds to a series of more or less straightforward questions. It has been known for some time that the scores we obtain in this way are not pure indicators of personality. Instead, any of several *response sets* may be operating, and these are likely to cloud the issue (Block, 1965). Some individuals agree to almost any characterization of them you offer, some reject them all. The former are called *yea-sayers*, or acquiescers, the latter *nay-sayers*. Some people are *extreme responders*; they tend to express their beliefs about themselves and other things strongly. Other people are more noncommittal and use the "neutral" or "don't know" response category more often than the other categories. *Social desirability* has been the bane of many test constructors: how do we know that individuals are not lying in order to make themselves look good? How do we know that individuals are not fooling themselves as well as us?

Other response sets have also been noted: tendencies to respond carelessly, to try to make a bad impression (out of a kind of test-taking perverseness), to answer consistently. Study after study has documented the potential threat that each of these may pose to a straightforward interpretation of data, and scales have been incorporated into the most prominent personality inventories in order to screen out the worst offenders. From time to time critics have alleged that paper-and-pencil tests may be explainable completely in terms of these stylistic (and substantively insignificant) sets (Berg, 1959), but careful analyses have consistently shown that this "nothing but" interpretation is far too extreme. Still, it is possible that the very high levels of stability in Table 1 are inflated by response sets.

Consider first the possibility that subjects are motivated to respond consistently from administration to administration: they recall how they answered questions the first time and repeat their performance on subsequent administrations despite real changes in their personality. This possibility is frequently advanced, but it becomes more and more implausible on examination. Why would people be so concerned with maintaining the appearance of consistency? A few subjects might be obsessed with maintaining an image, but it is hard to believe that nearly everyone in the sample would be (though that would be necessary to account for the observed coefficients). Further, even if they wanted to, is it likely that subjects *could* repeat their earlier performance? Informally, subjects often report that they do not even remember taking the test before—are we to believe that they somehow recall how they answered each particular question?

This deliberate consistency hypothesis is almost too implausible to entertain, so it is fortunate for us that it has already been tested. Woodruff and Birren (1972) retested a sample of individuals who had completed a personality measure twenty-five years before when they were in college. In addition to being given a simple readministration, the subjects were asked to fill out the questionnaire *as they believed they had filled it out twenty-five years earlier*. In terms of average level, the original responses were closer to the readministration responses than they were to the subject's recollections of the original responses. Woodruff (1983) demonstrated this even more forcefully when she examined the correlations between real and recalled responses. The correlation between original scores and later recollections was low and statistically non-significant. By contrast, there was a strong and highly significant correlation between original responses and personality as measured twenty-five years later. We get a more accurate picture of what people were like twenty-five years ago by asking what they are like today than by asking them to recall how they were; memories, it seems, are not as stable as personality.

A more plausible interpretation of a response set explanation goes something like this: when individuals take a test, they employ a characteristic set of response styles that operate like habits. Just as one never forgets how to ride a bicycle, so one may never forget the habits of test responding. When subjects take the test again years later, the same habits are activated and the same results obtained. Thus, there may be stability, but it is stability of response style, not personality.

This is not as strong an argument as it may at first seem. It might account for the convergence between scores on the same trait at two times, but it cannot explain the divergence between scores on different traits. The scales of the GZTS differ much more in content than in the response styles they are likely to elicit. Thus, the low correlations between unlike traits (for example, with sociability and thoughtfulness, $r = -.06$) are easily explained if content determines responses, but hard to explain if response sets determine responses. And if response sets do not account for scale scores at one time, they cannot account for the stability of scale scores across time. It is, however, still possible that stability is exaggerated by consistency of response habits.

Since response sets (including random responding, uncertainty, social desirability, and aquiescence) can be measured in the GZTS, we conducted empirical tests of this possibility (Costa, McCrae, and Arenberg, 1983). We found that there is indeed a certain consistency of response style across administrations, but it is less pronounced than the consistency of individual traits. And when we analyzed the data to eliminate the effects of this consistency, we found that the stability coefficients remained unchanged. Artifacts of response set do not account for stability of personality.

The Self-Concept and Stability

A much more interesting and reasonable rival hypothesis was suggested to us by Seymour Epstein, in a review he did of one of our earlier papers. Epstein drew attention to the distinction between personality and the self-concept, between what we are really like and what we believe we are like. He suggested that we may develop a view of ourselves early in adulthood and cling to that picture over the years, despite changes in our real nature. Rosenberg (1979, p. 58) expressed the same idea this way:

> The power and persistence of the self-consistency motive may be quite remarkable. People who have developed self-pictures early in life frequently continue to hold to these self-views long after the actual self has changed radically. . . . [T]he person who grows gruff and irritable with the passing years may still think of himself as "basically" kindly, cheerful,

and well-disposed; thus behavior which has become chronic is either un-recognized or is perceived as a temporary aberration from the true self.

Psychologists and sociologists have long known that we do have a self-concept, a theory of what we are like (Epstein, 1973), and that it seems to guide our behavior. It is this theory of ourselves that we draw upon when we are asked to describe ourselves, whether to a friend or on a questionnaire. There has been considerable dispute about how we develop a self-concept, whether or not self-concepts are accurate, and what the possibilities are for change in the self-concept during adulthood. According to one view, the self-concept may be crystal-lized early in life and remain unchanged thereafter.

Stories abound about middle-aged men who take up tennis or jogging after twenty years of inactivity and have to drastically revise their image of themselves as athletes. Normally they make these revisions fairly quickly. They have to; they cannot fool their bodies. But could they still imagine they were adventurous when they had lost their sense of daring? Could they still believe they were hostile when they had been mellowed by experience and age? Would anything in their intrapsychic or social experience *force* them to revise their self-concept, the way their exhaustion forces them to acknowledge the limits of their physical endurance?

Until we can answer these questions, the possibility remains that all we have demonstrated is the stability of self-concept. Further, this critique would apply equally to all studies, longitudinal and cross-sectional, that have relied on self-reports. In short, it would pull the rug out from under most of the claims of stability we have reviewed in this book and would allow the proponents of change to say, "See? People *do* change with age and with experience, just as we've told you. Only they don't *realize* they've changed. That's why you need clinicians to tell you what's really going on."

In this case we cannot rely on evidence from self-reports, since they are themselves in question. We have to get beyond self-reports, which are determined by the self-concept, if we want to see the agreement between the self-concept and the true personality. For this we must turn to someone else's assessment of personality, and in our case we had available personality ratings made by the husbands and wives of 281 of our subjects (McCrae and Costa, 1982). We assumed that spouses were reasonable judges of personality (we had data to support that assumption), but we also argued that the spouses would be much more able than the individuals themselves to detect any changes that age had brought. We may be blind to changes in ourselves, but we are not likely to overlook changes in other people whom we have to deal with on a daily basis.

By comparing self-reports with spouse ratings, we can get some idea of whether the self-concept has really been crystallized. Among young people the self-concept should still be quite accurate, a good reflection of what the person is really like. Consequently there should be good agreement between self-reports and spouse ratings among young couples. But if personality changes with age while the self-concept is frozen, self-reports will give increasingly inaccurate pictures of personality. Correspondingly, the agreement between self-reports and spouse ratings will become poorer and poorer. Among older couples there may be no agreement at all.

These would be the consequences if personality changed while the self-concept did not. When we examined the correlations between self and spouse for young, middle-aged, and elderly couples, however, we found no decrease in agreement with age. (In fact, the only significant difference is that there is more agreement—not less—about extraversion in older men.) This finding provides some powerful evidence that personality does not change and that crystallization of the self-concept cannot itself account for the correlations in Table 1.

There are other pieces of evidence as well. Clearly, the most straightforward way to disentangle personality from the self-concept would be to dispense with self-reports altogether and rely exclusively on ratings of personality. We do not yet have longitudinal data on spouse ratings of personality, but our cross-sectional analyses of spouse data confirm the conclusions we reached in Chapter 2: there is little difference between rated neuroticism, extraversion, and openness in young versus old men and women, and the small correlations that appear with age are almost certainly the results of generational differences or sample selection, rather than real change with age.

But other investigators have much better data on this question than we do. In particular, Jack Block (1971, 1981) has reported on a remarkable series of longitudinal studies conducted in Berkeley. Personality records have been kept on about 200 boys and girls over a period now approaching fifty years. These records include test scores, teachers' notes, biographical sketches, and many other documents. For each of the four time periods (junior high, senior high, the thirties, and the forties), independent judges reviewed these records and rated the subjects on the Q-Sort, a set of one hundred personality descriptors. Different judges were used for each time period, and yet when individuals were compared across time, remarkable evidence of stability in personality was found. When corrected for the unreliability of judges' ratings, the correlation of items often exceeded .50 over periods of twenty years and more.

In another study on the parents of these subjects, judges provided ratings across an interval of forty years, from ages thirty to seventy (Mussen et al., 1980). Again, despite the differences in judges and the unreliability of single-item scales, most of the ratings showed significant correlation across time. Stability of personality is not an individual's delusion; it is an objectively verifiable fact.

A Return to Retrospection

Earlier in this chapter, we mentioned that retrospection—asking individuals to recall how they were and how they have changed—was a simple but suspect method of examining stability or change in personality. We said that we could not be sure whether the reports would be accurate reflections of reality or distortions of memory. By now, however, we have a reasonable idea of what reality must have been like for most people: stability rather than change predominates when prospective longitudinal studies are conducted. So is there any reason to reconsider retrospective reports?

In fact, there is. They serve, of course, as one more source of data, one more way to bolster or cast doubt on our findings of constancy. But equally importantly, they let us know something about how individuals view their own lives. If most individuals were to claim that they had changed dramatically when all the evidence pointed to the opposite conclusion, this would suggest that memory does indeed play tricks on us, and the function of these tricks would be of considerable interest. It might also explain why critics find the notion of stability in personality so counterintuitive.

Most people, in fact, can point to aspects of themselves that have changed in the past few years, and the reader may have been protesting on the basis of these exceptions throughout this book. But three things should be borne in mind in considering this kind of evidence. First, in one important sense retrospection is different from any of the kinds of studies we have reviewed. Statistics are usually interpreted in terms of individual differences; that is, they compare one individual with others. Saying that a person is warm means, in a certain sense, that she is warmer than most other people; saying that warmth does not change with age means that she will continue to be warmer than most people throughout life. But if we ask the individual is she has changed, she will be making comparisons between herself as she was and herself as she is now. She is likely to be far more sensitive to these changes than we are. We might find that she has risen from the fifty-fifth to the fifty-eighth percentile in warmth—a change we would call trivial. From her perspective, however, this change may be extremely important and the contrast very vivid.

Second, as perceptual psychologists would remind us, our attention is attracted by movement and contrast, not by stability and sameness. If a person is unchanged in characteristic levels of anxiety, hostility, assertiveness, excitement-seeking, and openness to feelings and values, but has changed in gregariousness, he or she is much more likely to notice and remark on the change in that one element than on the stability in the other six. Our prediction of stability would be confirmed in 85 percent of the cases, but we would be judged wrong because of the one exception. Stability is not absolute, but it is far more pervasive than many people realize.

Finally, the question of sampling arises again. Readers of this book, and life-span developmental psychologists, are not representative of humanity in general. They are, for the most part, intelligent, perceptive, and curious individuals. And almost certainly they are interested in seeing what changes age and experience bring to them. In short, they begin with a bias toward finding change and the mental faculties to spot it, no matter how subtle or small it may be. Most people are not like that.

We first discovered this when we began to investigate the so-called midlife crisis (Costa and McCrae, 1978). At that time we assumed we would find abundant evidence of a crisis; we simply wanted to document it. (See Chapter 6 for a fuller discussion of this study.) At the end of a standard questionnaire, we asked that subjects simply comment on the ways in which they felt they had changed in the past ten years. Subject after subject returned the questionnaire with words to the effect of "no changes worth mentioning." A few subjects did find some change to comment on; the great majority did not. And if we rephrased the question and asked, "Do you think you are a completely different sort of person now from the person you were when you were twenty-five years old?" virtually everyone over forty would strongly disagree.

One last piece of evidence should be mentioned here, also based on retrospection. Reichard, Livson, and Peterson (1962), in one of the seminal books on personality and aging, interviewed a number of retired men to find out how they were adapting to old age and retirement. The interviewers spent a good deal of time taking life histories of their subjects so that they could note patterns of adjustment across the life span. Their conclusion? "The histories of our aging workers suggest that their personality characteristics changed very little throughout their lives" (p. 163).

Implications: Planning for the Future

Imagine the chaos that would result if personality were *not* stable! How could we commit ourselves to marriage if the qualities we loved in our spouse were subject to change at any time? Who would go to the trouble of completing medical school without the faith that he or she would still be interested in medicine years later? How could we vote for politicians if their past diligence and conscientiousness were not a token of their future performance? On what basis would we decide to retire early and move to Florida if we thought that at any moment we might become compulsive workers with boundless energy?

With the exception of those closest to us (whom we may never give up trying to change), we expect people to stay just as they are. Good or bad, we want them to be dependable and predictable, so that we can count on them in making plans for our own future. They feel the same way about us; one of the explanations for stability is the social pressure applied to keep everyone in his or her place. We can shape our own lives, attain our dreams, and find fulfillment for ourselves only if we can make realistic plans for the future. Since so much of life depends on our interactions with others, being able to guess how they are likely to respond years from now is essential.

The same is even more true for ourselves. Continuity in personality is a requirement for planning a viable future; it is also a source of the sense of identity. When, in Erikson's last stage, we review our lives and take stock of what we have been and done, we must do so to some extent in terms of our enduring dispositions. If we are extraverts, we will cherish the friendships we have cultivated over the years; if introverts, we will appraise the tasks accomplished. Lifelong dreams of writing poetry or fostering a family or dominating an industry make sense only in terms of the basic needs and traits they express. The constancy of personality is a unifying thread that gives meaning to our lives.

*   *   *

Once we begin to think in terms of stability, it becomes increasingly intuitive. Our parents and grandparents do not seem to change, although our understanding of them may alter greatly as we grow up. History tells us that Beethoven was a rebel at age twenty and at age fifty, that Chairman Mao did not grow conservative with age. Hospital and prison records show that tendencies toward mental illness and antisocial behavior are dishearteningly stable. One begins to wonder how the idea of adult development ever arose to begin with.

But are we perhaps missing the whole point? Granted, emotional, interpersonal, and experiential styles may be relatively fixed, but are these the real cores of personality? Or are they instead peripheral characteristics whose stability is no more remarkable or noteworthy than is stability in color of eyes or size of feet? Perhaps what is needed is not a different form of personality test or a different personality rater, but a wholly different conception of personality in which it is seen not as trait but as process. Perhaps processes change with age.

Chapter

5

A Different View: Ego Psychologies and Projective Methods

The finding of stability in discrete traits we have discussed is not likely to be impressive to those who think of personality in terms other than traits. Behaviorists in general do not think of personality at all. They are interested in studying—and especially in controlling—behavior, and traits offer little promise of a way to reshape behavior; in fact, they may represent the greatest resistance to change.

Our concern in this chapter, however, will be with a different set of approaches to personality: the psychodynamic psychologies that see personality not as a collection of traits, each operating more or less independently to influence behavior, but as an *organization* of needs, motives, dispositions, habits, and abilities, an organization generally thought to be in the service of certain overarching goals. Depending on the version of psychodynamic theory, these goals might be set by biological instincts, the dictates of culture, or the individual's own experience and convictions.

In this chapter we will also turn to an evaluation of projective methods, a form of personality assessment frequently advocated by ego psychologists. Do they make satisfactory substitutes for self-report inventories, or do they provide unique insights? Or does a careful consideration lead to a rejection of projective techniques altogether?

Dynamic or Ego Psychologies

To the student of personality theory, it may seem strange to group together the theories of Freud, Jung, Rogers, Murray, Loevinger, Maslow—even Allport—as ego psychologies (in contrast to

71

trait psychologies), but from a certain perspective it is perfectly reasonable. All these writers assume that individuals possess a variety of different and potentially conflicting tendencies, and all assume that the major business of personality theory is to explain how and why all these impulses are channeled and directed into the routine, purposeful, or occasionally irrational behavior we engage in or the stream of consciousness we experience. Although the term *self* is sometimes used, *ego* is the word most frequently chosen to represent the aspect of the mind or personality that does the organizing.

We cannot hope in a few pages to provide adequate sketches of the theories we will be discussing—dozens of textbooks in personality theory do that already. We would, however, like to try to indicate some of the features they share that set them apart from trait theories. For our purposes we will emphasize the similarities of ego psychologies and minimize the profound differences, which are perhaps better known.

For Freud (1933), the ego develops as a mediator between fierce and primitive instinctual impulses (the id), punitive prohibitions internalized in childhood (the superego), and the social realities of the world. It operates through a series of tricks called defense mechanisms and is ultimately very much at the mercy of the powers it attempts to control. This division of the psyche is at least as old as Plato, who wrote of appetite, passion, and reason as the elements of human nature and who held that man's goal was the harmonious balancing of these parts. Freud's framework also seems to parallel the different emphases that have distinguished psychological schools in this century, since it acknowledges the importance of inborn tendencies and environmental pressures, as well as the capacity of cognitive processes—reason and individual choice—to moderate both these influences. In short, it seems likely that every complete psychology will have to deal with these issues in some form; one of Freud's major contributions was to formulate the twentieth-century version of an age-old question. Many of the important personality theorists have made their primary contributions by modifying previous descriptions of the nature or significance of one of the three structures.

Murray (1938) uses the same general scheme of dynamic control, but changes the cast of characters considerably. Instead of describing primitive impulses, he endows human beings with a range of needs, some inborn, some acquired; and he proposes that the ego is a strong agent, not a figurehead, in most people, who use reason rather than defense to come up with solutions, compromises, plans, and schedules. Murray also proposed that the superego, the agent of morality within the individual, is not wholly unconscious and immutable. He felt that maturation, or what we would today call *moral development* (Kohlberg, 1971), was not only possible but the general rule.

Allport, Murray's contemporary at Harvard, developed two theories of personality, which he never clearly integrated. He is perhaps best known for his work as a trait psychologist (1966), but he also developed a dynamic theory of personality (1955). He emphasized the purposeful nature of human conduct and the significance of overarching goals, or *propriate strivings*, that guide and organize life.

Maslow (1954) was also a motivational theorist; his major thesis was that there are broad classes of needs that organize individuals' lives. The history of satisfaction of these needs determines the person's progress through a set sequence of motivations, ranging from the physical through the social to the transcendental needs of the self-actualizing person. In the writings of humanists like Maslow, the element of conflict, central to Freudian thought, is minimized and characterizes maladjusted or neurotic individuals rather than the natural human condition.

Developmental Sequences

In addition to their similar emphasis on the process of resolving conflicts and satisfying needs, most of the major theorists of personality explicitly include theories of human development. Some, like Freud, with his psychosexual stages, or Maslow, with his motivational levels, deal with changes in the nature of the motivational tendencies, the forces that are to be channeled. Others concentrate on growth in the structures that organize the fundamental tendencies. Most assert that higher processes such as reason, empathy, and self-control allow mastery of raw impulses in ever more sophisticated ways.

Loevinger (1966) has proposed a theory of what she calls ego development. She distinguishes six stages, each qualitatively different from the others. The impulsive stage is characteristic only of infants and perhaps of severely disturbed adults, but the other stages are found at all ages. Although each person is supposed to go through the same sequence of stages, many do not outgrow the early ones. In theory, the process is irreversible: once mature, one can never again think and act in a truly immature way.

The stages Loevinger proposes are perhaps most easily characterized in terms of socialization. Individuals in the early stages are preconventional; they want their own way and have few scruples about how they get it. The rules of society are for them merely obstacles to their desires, and although they may follow rules when they know they would be caught otherwise, they have no real allegiance to them. Individuals at the conventional stages—where most adults function—have a very different attitude. They believe wholeheartedly in the need for and wisdom of rules, as determined by religion, law, or local standards of taste and etiquette. *Conforming* persons do what they are told to without much question; they follow rituals and forms without necessarily understanding them, and they are motivated by the desire to maintain the good opinion of their fellows. *Conscientious* men and women, in the next higher stage, are also loyal to their country and faith, but are more thoughtful in their interpretation. They are guided by principles, not customs, and are beholden mostly to their own consciences. At the same time, the principles they follow are dictated by society, and they do not venture to question them.

At the two highest stages of ego development are individuals who can be considered postconventional. They have internalized the principles of their social environment, but they have also transcended them. They, too, are guided by principles, but by principles of their own devising; and they are not unwilling to defy social customs that conflict with what they believe is a higher law. Great social reformers and founders of religions are usually at this level, but so are many ordinary individuals who do not choose to make a career out of their ethical opinions.

This description of Loevinger's stages is, of course, a great oversimplification, in part because it fails to show the importance of emotional and cognitive changes that accompany the moral development. The form of thought necessary to articulate one's own moral principle is far more sophisticated than that required to say, "I want it!" Sensitivity to others' feelings or to one's own unspoken fears or desires is also a far cry from the raw lust or rage that can characterize individuals at the lower ego levels. Progressive levels of ego development, then, are characterized by increasing complexity, differentiation, and integration of thoughts, feelings, and actions.

Dynamic Dispositions

Dynamic theorists often prefer to speak of needs or motives rather than of traits. Motives and needs are dynamic in the sense that they drive behavior, urging us on to do whatever is necessary to achieve certain goals. Some needs, like the need for oxygen, are universal; others, like the need for achievement, characterize only some people or vary in the degree to which they are important to individuals. Motivational psychologists are concerned with the universal ways in which needs are experienced, acquired, and expressed, while personality theorists are generally interested in identifying the needs or motives that typify or characterize an individual, usually in contrast to others. Thus we say that Smith is high in the need for achievement, whereas Jones is low in the need for achievement but high in the need for affiliation.

If this description of needs sounds familiar, it is because it is very similar to the definition previously offered for traits. The items in questionnaires that purport to measure needs—the Edwards Personal Preference Schedule, for example, or the Jackson Personality Research Form—look very much like items in questionnaires that measure traits, and some theorists, like Guilford (1959), regard motives as a class of traits.

The only real problem with this conceptualization is that it suggests that there is a clear boundary between motivational and other traits. The distinction between motivational and temperamental traits or between adaptive and expressive traits (Allport, 1937) is in many respects artificial. Traits as we measure them seem to form a syndrome of motives, moods, expressive and adaptive behavior, and attitudes. The hostile individual, for example, may be high in the need for aggression, often experience the emotion of anger, have a gruff tone of voice, use direct attack as a way of solving problems, and believe that people will always do their best to cause you trouble. The person high in openness to aesthetics may desire to collect art, enjoy beautiful objects, have artistic handwriting, take lessons to learn painting, and believe the government should support the arts. Traits, then, can be said to have motivational as well as other components. Recall that *disposition* is another word for both *trait* and *motive*. Given the similarities between the two, it seems somewhat silly to decry the static nature of traits.

Contrasting Traits with Ego Processes

Trait theories do share with dynamic theories a concern for motivation. But in other respects the two approaches differ, and it is important to consider these differences in judging whether personality changes with age. The most significant differences have to do with the role of ego processes in resolving conflicts and organizing behavior over time.

Conflict and Its Resolution

Dynamic theories of personality tend to emphasize the interaction of the elements they postulate. Freud's instinctive urges are forever battling against irrational prohibitions and rational restraints for expression. Each bit of behavior we observe, each passing thought in our mind is held to be the end result of this perpetual conflict. At one moment the forces of the ego are in control; the next, a slip of the tongue or pen reveals a momentary breach in the defensive armor. Rarely can any behavior be understood as the expression of any single internal tendency. Instead, drives may merge together (as sex and aggression do in sadism) or may be transformed by defense mechanisms into their opposite or may represent a compromise between the dictates of the superego and the cravings of the id. It hardly comes as a surprise to Freudians when personality traits do not predict behavior very well, since behavior is a function of the constantly changing relative strengths of a host of actively competing forces.

As usual, Freudian theory presents this view in its extreme form, holding that *all* behavior is defensive and that conflict is inevitable. Later theorists, like Rogers and Maslow, took a less grim view of the human condition, believing that conflict was not inherent in human nature. But many personality theories recognize the need to explain the mechanisms by which conflicts between impulses or principles are resolved when they do arise.

At each moment we are capable of acting and experiencing in only a very limited way. We are not at liberty to express our assertiveness or indulge our anxiety continually, even if we would like to. We are limited by the opportunities the environment presents, the demands that society and the persons we interact with place on us, and sometimes the competing pressures of imcompatible traits: excitement-seeking bids us to drive faster, anxiety urges us to slow down. It is obvious that choices must be made—consciously, unconsciously, or by habit—and it is clear that these choices are not, by and large, random. Sane, mature individuals are not buffeted by internal and external pressures like leaves in the wind. With more or less success, they coordinate their behavior and routinely resolve conflicts. The mechanisms for resolving conflict are an important part of the ego.

For psychoanalysts, conflict is usually resolved through the use of defense mechanisms (A. Freud, 1936). Wishes or memories that would create too much guilt or anxiety because of their conflict with internalized prohibitions are repressed, transformed, or disguised. The individual is not even aware that a conflict exists, except when the transformations fail or lead to neurotic symptoms. Whether or not one accepts the accounts offered by analysts, it is certainly true that individuals do learn to control their impulses. Sometimes suppression—deliberate and conscious inhibition—is involved, but often the offending desires never reach consciousness. Children cry when they do not get what they want; adults may feel frustrated, but it rarely occurs to them to cry.

Murray and Kluckhohn (1953) describe a number of more rational ways to resolve conflicts between tendencies. Using reason, foresight, and self-control, the individual with a strong ego is able to choose between competing courses of action, resist temptations that would lead to undesirable consequences, and resolve the conflicting claims of social pressures, personal preferences, and external necessity. Resolving conflicts need not mean the application of rigid self-control. There are usually opportunities for compromise or for creative solutions. Two needs may be fused (that is, both may be satisfied by the same behavior, as when a neurotic extravert talks about his imaginary illnesses), or one may be used in the service of another, as when a person closed to values uses her assertiveness to force a conservative position on a group.

Temporal Organization

Another way to resolve conflicts is to allow each tendency expression at a different time. By creating—and sticking to—routines or *schedules* (as Murray calls them) we can manage to satisfy all or most of our needs on a regular basis. Organizing behavior in time is an essential and distinctive feature of ego processes.

Consider for a moment the course of a typical day. We get up, eat breakfast, go to work, apply ourselves to the necessary tasks, take breaks, talk to our co-workers, eat lunch and perhaps read a book, go back to work, and so on. Trait theorists would make certain predictions about this collection of behavior: for example, introverts are more likely to read at lunch time and less likely to spend a good deal of their day in social conversation; people high in neuroticism may wake up tired, get angry about the work expected of them, overeat at lunch; open people are more likely to spend their working hours on tasks like writing, teaching college, or doing research; closed people will more likely be attending to business and following strict routines (Costa, Fozard, and McCrae, 1977).

But although information about traits can be extremely useful in predicting specifics of behavior, it cannot, by itself, account for the structured flow or temporal sequence of behavior. These are ego functions, as important in shaping the life course as in managing daily routines. In addition to schedules, Murray proposed the notion of *serials*, programs of action extended over time and intended to achieve long-range goals. Attending college and law school, working in a law firm, beginning one's own practice, and running for local office may all be steps toward a political career; only with planned and coordinated efforts, pursued diligently over a long period of time, can this end be achieved. Murray holds that the selection and pursuit of realistic goals over extended periods of the life span is a major task of the ego.

Individual Differences in Ego Processes

Trait theory does not deal with the processes—instrumental learning, formal reasoning, creative planning, defensive distortion—by which behavior and experience are molded on a moment-to-moment basis. But even though dynamic theorists make these processes central to their theories, most are also concerned with characterizing individuals. People differ in the needs, values, and goals that must be organized and harmonized by the ego, but they also differ in the ways in which the ego goes about its task of coordination. It is not simply that people make plans for the future: some plan wisely, some poorly, some hardly at all. Individual differences in ego processes are an important issue in personality theory.

Loevinger's theory of ego stages is a clear example. Men and women in the lower stages of development are subject to strong and primitive impulses and tend to express them immediately. Because their ego functioning is undeveloped, they cannot resolve conflicts effectively or set up efficient schedules. In the long run they are unable to satisfy many needs, at least without provoking guilt or reprisals from others. Persons with higher levels of ego development have far more sensitive and sophisticated ways of integrating their needs and values. On the other hand, the lives of individuals with high ego levels are correspondingly more complex, and they are troubled by abstract problems to which persons with low ego levels are oblivious. Thus, high ego development does not necessarily mean greater satisfaction or happiness (McCrae and Costa, 1983).

Other theories of individual differences in ego functioning are more attentive to overall adjustment. *Ego strength* is a characteristic discussed by a number of psychoanalytic writers, who generally define it as the ability of the individual to manage successfully the competing forces of instinctual demands, internal prohibitions, and social reality. Murray uses the term to describe characteristics needed to lead a well-ordered life. People thought to be low in ego strength are less intelligent, more ethnocentric, and generally more prone to many kinds of psychopathology (Barron, 1980).

Block (1965) distinguished two dimensions of ego functioning.

Ego resiliency is defined as the individual's ability to adapt to new demands. Individuals high in ego resiliency are resourceful and flexible; those who are low are touchy, moody, and uncomfortable in their world. *Ego control*, a second dimension, is seen in characteristic levels of impulse control. Overcontrolled individuals are overconforming, narrow in interests, and interpersonally distant; undercontrolled people are spontaneous, inclined toward immediate gratification of impulses, and willing to act in new and untried ways.

Traits and Metatraits?

Concepts like ego level, ego strength, and ego control are intended to describe the functioning of the ego in different individuals, but as enduring characteristics they resemble traits much more than ego processes. One way to distinguish them from more mundane traits is to grant them the status of superordinate traits or *metatraits*. These are the enduring dispositions that govern the expression and integration of other dispositions. Loevinger (1966) comes close to this formulation when she calls ego level the "master trait."

But as we begin to examine the idea of metatraits closely, their distinctness begins to evaporate. Block's description of ego resiliency makes it sound very much like low vulnerability to stress, and ego undercontrol seems to resemble a combination of impulsiveness, extraversion, and openness to experience. Barron's ego-strength scale is known to correlate with measures of maladjustment and neuroticism. And Loevinger's master trait of ego level is strongly related to intelligence as well as to personality (McCrae and Costa, 1980). A study we conducted in Boston employed the sentence completions of 240 men to examine ego levels using Loevinger's own instrument. The scores we obtained were correlated with our measures of personality and intelligence. We found, as she has repeatedly, that there is a marked correlation with IQ (about .50), showing that higher ego levels are more often found in more intelligent people. But we also found that there was a significant correlation with openness to experience, even when we controlled for intelligence. More open people are rated as being more mature in the Loevinger system.

One interpretation of these conceptual and empirical correspondences would suggest that traits and metatraits are not really distinct. The same traits that are organized by the ego are responsible for the individual differences in the way the ego organizes them. Intelligence is a trait, but it also modifies the ways other traits are expressed: introverts read books, intelligent introverts read difficult books. Again, anxiety is a trait, but the disposition to anxiety may disrupt the efficient functioning of other traits. Test anxiety, for example, may lead to poor performance despite high intelligence.

If these speculations are correct, we do not need to introduce new traits to explain differences in ego organization or the resulting differences in the life structure. Instead, we must recognize that in order to describe fully the significance of a trait, we must not only specify the behaviors and feelings associated with it, but also identify the effects the trait has on the organization of other traits.

The other side of this interpretation is that in inferring traits we ought to look not simply at specific behaviors, but at the whole pattern of the individual's life. And this is precisely what we advocated in Chapter 3.

Developmental Changes in Ego Processes

If the essence of personality is the organization and integration of experience and behavior, the most important question about age and personality would be what happens to the major ego functions with age. It is in this context, perhaps, that the issue of growth or decline in personality makes most sense. After all, what do we mean by growth in personality? It is easy to see that becoming taller or more intelligent is growth, but how does personality grow? Although we assumed in Chapter 2 that any change in the average level of a trait could be interpreted as either growth or decline, in fact it would have been difficult to interpret an increase in introversion or openness to aesthetic experiences in these terms. Not all changes represent growth or decline.

But we could probably make a good case for the contention that there is a natural direction of growth in ego functioning. Loevinger suggests as much in her developmental stages, as does Erikson (1950) in his stages of psychosocial development. Many other writers have also proposed criteria of psychological maturity that could properly be seen as growth in personality and would generally be considered attributes of ego functioning. Bühler mentions formulation of a stable identity, willingness to assume responsibility, ability to form significant and lasting attachments to others, self-acceptance, emotional security, and commitment to life goals (Bühler, Keith-Spiegel, and Thomas, 1973).

Most of us would agree that these are signs of maturity, and we would probably suspect that adults possess more of them than do adolescents. But does maturity increase with age once we have become adults? Or do older individuals regress to more primitive ways of resolving conflicts, dealing with others, and organizing their activities?

If the argument we developed above is correct—if ego character-istics are determined by such traits as anxiety, depression, warmth, and openness to ideas—it would follow that there ought not to be major changes in the functioning of the ego across the adult life span, since the traits that determine it are themselves stable.

Consider the case of ego development. If individuals continue to mature in the period of adulthood, the ego levels of older individuals should be higher than those of younger individuals. But we know that ego level is related to the traits of intelligence and openness and that both of these are generally stable in adulthood. We would predict, then, that there should be no changes in ego level. And cross-sectional data from the Boston sample clearly confirm that prediction (McCrae and Costa, 1980). Longitudinal studies have shown that the predicted changes in ego development are seen as individuals move from childhood to adolescence, but there is no evidence of change after adulthood is reached. If ego level is indeed the master trait, this is one more evidence of stability at all levels of personality.

At this point, none of these studies can be considered conclusive. It is much harder to describe the organization of elements than the elements themselves. Additionally there is no consensus on what properties of the ego we should be measuring: is control of impulses the key, or the arrangement of attitudes and beliefs? Should we be concerned with the normal daily functioning of individuals, with their responses to crisis situations, or with their long-range plans? Or must we develop a battery of tests to consider each of these separately?

And what kind of tests? It may be that individuals, although able to report adequately on emotional reactions or vocational prefer-ences, are incapable of judging the more profound styles that tie together all these discrete elements. Perhaps an analysis of a deeper level of personality is needed. Projective tests are supposed to give a picture of the deeper layers of personality, and we will shortly review what they have to tell us about age and personality. But just as we were compelled to describe the rationale and evaluate the efficacy of self-report measures in Chapter 3, so now we must do the same to lay the groundwork for an evaluation of projectives.

Projective and Clinical Assessments of Personality

For reasons partly historical and partly theoretical, psychologists of the dynamic school have usually preferred evaluations of per-sonality based on something other than self-reports. The first and most common argument offered against self-report assessments is that individuals may not be aware of important aspects of their personality and may in fact systematically distort their perceptions and reports of themselves. This is a perfectly reasonable point of view for Freudians, who locate the variables of real interest in the unconscious. We cannot expect individuals to report accurately the ways in which they deceive themselves and try to deceive others; yet, according to psychoanalysts, these defenses are among the most important aspects of personality.

As a result clinicians and researchers have devised a number of methods of assessing personality indirectly. Most of these tests are called *projective*, from the belief that the individual projects his or her personality unwittingly into the task. Asked to describe a picture, individuals probably imagine that their responses tell about what they see. The psychologist, however, believes that the responses tell about the subject. A variety of techniques have been used to outsmart the subject in this way. The individuals being assessed may be asked to give associations to words, report what they see in inkblots, make up stories to accompany the cards of the Thematic Apperception Test (TAT), draw pictures, or write completions for unfinished sentences.

The scoring of these materials is, of course, very different from summing up the items on a scale. A judge (usually human, but occasionally a computer) must consider the subject's production in the light of some set of rules developed to judge the characteristic of interest. Sometimes the rules are quite specific; sometimes they require extensive intuition. The scoring system may be based on the empirical strategy of contrasting the responses of one group with those of another, or it may be derived from purely theoretical considerations. Psychoanalytically oriented researchers often propose scoring systems based on the presumed symbolic significance of responses. There is a strong tradition of assessing needs through the TAT on the assumption that the concerns of the story's hero are those of the story's creator (McClelland, 1980; Murray, 1938). A story about long struggles leading to a successful career, for instance, might be interpreted as evidence of a high need for achievement.

Many dynamic psychologists do not take so extreme a view as the Freudian belief that the interesting aspects of personality are unconscious. These dynamic psychologists attach more importance to the events of conscious life and observable behavior, or they assume that individuals may have more insight into their own motivations than Freud credited them with. They have other grounds for preferring projective tests to self-report methods.

McClelland (1980) distinguishes between what he calls *operant* and *respondent* tests. The former consist of materials—a picture, a blank sheet of paper, a sentence fragment—that the subject can organize and interpret for him- or herself; the pictures on TAT cards are the primary example. Respondent tests are exemplified by questionnaire items, in which the subject must respond within a strictly limited number of alternative ways to a fixed set of items. McClelland objects that this regimentation, which makes scoring of respondent tests so convenient, introduces an artificiality. An older individual, for example, might find all the items in a test designed for college students irrelevant to her, though if urged she would still fill it out. What would the responses mean in that case? Operant tests are not subject to this criticism. The subject can always *make* a picture relevant by choosing what elements to respond to or by creating a story that goes beyond the picture toward whatever concerns he or she has.

Loevinger makes a similar point in defending her choice of a sentence-completion test to measure ego development. What is of primary interest, she maintains, is not so much what the person decides as how he or she makes the decision. Asking the subject to complete stems (for example, "What I like best about being a man is . . . ") gives the researcher an opportunity to observe how the subject will structure and organize responses, free from the promptings of the investigator. Since it is the processing of the ego that Loevinger wants to measure and since most situations in life present the same ambiguity as pictures or half-formed sentences, it can be argued that tests that simulate these conditions should give the best picture of the ego at work. In effect, such tests provide samples of ego functioning, rather than reports about how the individual thinks he or she is.

There are thus two major lines of argument about the superiority of projective tests over questionnaires. The first holds that the real personality is hidden from the subject and can only be inferred indirectly from signs and symbols that the trained psychologist must interpret. The second supposes that, while not necessarily hidden, the personality is best assessed by observation as it works in an unstructured situation. Both would concur in the belief that answers to personality inventories are largely irrelevant.

Problems in Projective Methods

Forty years ago, both of these were reasonable arguments. By now, however, we have had time to think them through a bit more and, more important, to test some of the propositions empirically. The results are sobering.

In the first place, although the limitations of objective tests are widely known, there are also grave problems with projective tests.

When we ask subjects to draw a picture or tell a story, their artistic abilities are likely to be much more in evidence than their intrapsychic dynamics. Under the naive assumption that the hero of the story represents the personality of the storyteller, we would have to infer that novelists, who are capable of describing a huge range of human characters, have multiple personalities. Verbal skill, motivation, and perceptual problems (common in the elderly) all have a much greater impact on projective responses than they do on objective test results. Indeed, projective tests may be most valuable as samples of cognitive behavior, not personality.

A second problem is the unreliability of projective tests. Personality is supposed to be consistent across time and situations; it is, almost by definition, that which endures as the momentary pressures of the environment and the body vary (Maddi, 1980). The specific behaviors may well change, but the psychologist should be able to infer the underlying unity throughout the changes. It seems reasonable to expect that the projective test results, which allegedly mirror personality, would show the same degree of consistency across different forms of the test or at different times. This is the criterion of reliability, and it has always proven to be a sore spot in projective testing. TAT stories change from one time to another, and so do the scores derived from them (Winter and Stewart, 1977), perhaps because needs change as a result of their expression on the test (Atkinson, Bongort, and Price, 1977).

But if the expression of needs is subject to such marked fluctuations, we have no way of knowing whether the responses we obtain on the first test are characteristic of the individual or simply a reflection of the immediate situation. TAT measures may be accurate reflections of the *state* of the individual, but if they are not reliable over time they are poor indicators of characteristic *traits* of the individual. The same argument, of course, also applies to projective tests of processes other than needs: defenses, complexes, attitudes, cognitive styles. Demonstrable retest reliability is essential to the measurement of individual characteristics, and few projective tests meet even minimal standards of reliability.

Third, there are significant problems with the idea of personality sampling. A questionnaire item that asks "Are you often irritable and angry?" requires the subject to review his or her behavior over a period of months and to estimate the typical level of this state. To the extent that the person is able to weigh accurately his or her recollections, this item gives an average based on thousands of hours of living in a wide range of situations. By contrast, observing the responses of the individual to an inkblot or sentence fragment gives only a tiny sample of behaviors and all within the thoroughly artificial situation of a psychological testing session. One of the recent conclusions from the trait-consistency controversy is that any single instance of behavior is likely to be a very poor indicator of the average level (Epstein, 1979); if we really want samples of ego functioning, we must plan to spend a great deal more time and effort than we currently do.

Finally, and most compelling, the results of careful research studies using projective tests to measure traits or predict outcomes have had uniformly disappointing results. When clinical tests are used, experts frequently fail even to agree on how to score them. In a detailed review of studies on projective tests conducted between 1950 and 1965, Suinn and Oskamp (1969) conclude, "There are only a few things which the clinician can predict from these personality tests with confidence that his judgments are being made on a scientific basis. The remainder of his predictive work is still based on faith or on theory rather than on evidence" (p. 117).

Conscious versus Unconscious Elements

One of the most intriguing aspects of Suinn and Oskamp's review is the consistent finding that the most nearly valid tests were those that agreed most closely with self-report.

Sentence-completion tests, for example, which come closest to direct self-reports, are among the better validated projective tests. Rotter and Rafferty (1950) constructed a sentence-completion test of maladjustment that was significantly correlated with both clinical judgments and self-reports of adjustment. In our study of ego level and openness to experience (McCrae and Costa, 1980), we examined responses to Loevinger's sentence-completion stems for evidence of openness (without knowledge of how subjects had rated themselves). We judged subjects as *open* when we found statements showing flexible views of rules, rejection of traditional sex roles, intrinsic interest in experience, or playfulness. When we compared our judgments with the self-reports of openness the same subjects had given us, we found agreement in 78 percent of the cases.

But projective assessments frequently fail to agree with self-reports. In these cases, there is usually also little agreement with any other criterion of importance, such as suicide, sexual orientation, or improvement in therapy. And fascinating as the symbolic interpretations of the Freudians are, there is simply no good evidence that they are correct.

What all of this suggests to us is that the unconscious level of personality either cannot be measured by projectives or does not have much influence on human conduct. No one who has read Freud or Jung could fail to appreciate the marvelous insight that there are levels of the mind that operate by a logic different from that of our waking consciousness; that these are more characteristic of children than of adults; that they appear in dreams, in artistic productions, in psychotic delusions, and in culturally shared myths; and that the primitive ways of thinking we have inherited from our evolutionary ancestors often appear in them in undisguised form. The data collected over the past fifty years, however, have convinced us that these curious relics of our past have relatively little to do with our daily life or with such important outcomes as mental illness, response to stress, or political beliefs.

Projective Testing and the Stability of Personality

Let us summarize the argument so far and then proceed to a more specific consideration of the relation between projectively assessed personality and aging. We have considered the reasons for preferring projective tests to self-reports and have rejected them. Some projective tests aim at a deeper level of personality, but that deeper level, if it is indeed tapped by such tests, does not appear to have much influence on important aspects of personality. Some projective tests aim to sample the ego, to judge it by its spontaneous functioning in an unstructured situation. But there is strong reason to believe that the samples obtained are generally inadequate and that when they approach adequacy they simply duplicate information that could more easily have been obtained by direct questioning.

We might, therefore, dismiss projective testing altogether and decline to review a literature based on such faulty instruments. We have noted that sentence-completion tests, the most reliable of projectives, show no cross-sectional relation to age in adulthood (McCrae and Costa, 1980). However, it is worthwhile to consider some examples of aging and personality research using projective techniques, if only as a way of illustrating the points already made.

Cross-sectional studies of inkblot responses do in fact show a regular progression of age-related changes. Old people make fewer and more concrete descriptions of what they see and tend to give global responses instead of picking out minor details (Kahana, 1978). Both cross-sectional and longitudinal studies (Ames, 1965) have verified this tendency; but before concluding that here at last is evidence of personality change, we must bear in mind that the Rorshach is used to assess cognition and perception as well as personality. There is no doubt that there are age-related changes in learning, memory, perceptual closure, and visual acuity, and these, rather than personality change, may well account for the age differences. Caldwell made that argument as long ago as 1954, and Eisdorfer (1963) provided some strong evidence in favor of it. When he matched old and young subjects on cognitive abilities as measured by the Wechsler Adult Intelligence Scales (WAIS), he found no differences in Rorshach responses.

Some of the most interesting data come from the TAT. In a cross-sectional national survey, Veroff and his colleagues (1960) found declines in need for achievement in men, and in needs for affiliation and power in women. The magnitude of change was—as usual—quite small, and we cannot rule out generational differences as the source of even these small differences.

Gutmann (1970) uses TAT cards for his research, but claims to find much larger changes by scoring for different variables. He is interested in the concept of ego mastery and has distinguished three kinds of responses: active, passive, and magical mastery. Cross-cultural longitudinal studies show that as men age they pass from a stage of active mastery (in which TAT heroes forcefully tackle the problems of their world) to a stage of passive mastery (in which they acquiesce in the demands of the environment) and then to a stage of magical mastery (in which problems are denied or wished away). Gutmann's description of ego mastery style as a measure of coping style or adaptational ability suggests that it should have some consequences for the ways in which older people adapt to stress.

Objective studies of age and coping do not show any tendency for older people to use magical denial in solving real-life problems (McCrae, 1982a). In two studies, BLSA subjects were asked to describe how they had coped with recent stresses, chosen either by us or by the subjects themselves. Using a self-report checklist of ways of coping, we assigned them scores on twenty-eight different coping mechanisms, including rational action, distraction, denial of affect, intellectual denial, and passivity. We found age differences in the kinds of stress older people faced—generally more threats to health and fewer occupational and family challenges—but when the responses had been corrected for these differences only two consistent findings emerged. Younger men and women were more likely than middle-aged and older ones to indulge in escapist fantasy and hostile reactions. There was no evidence whatsoever that magical solutions were chosen by the elderly.

Gutmann himself is careful to point out that the progression he posits occurs on the level of fantasy, not of reality. Among the Druze, in particular, the old men are respected as leaders and decision makers; they are anything but passive.

So it seems that neither self-reports nor direct observations of behavior show parallels to the developmental sequence inferred by Gutmann from TAT responses. Perhaps these changes are due to cognitive or perceptual shifts, or perhaps they are changes in a deeper level of personality. In any case, they appear to have little impact on social or emotional functioning.

Finally, a few longitudinal studies using the TAT speak to the issue of individual stability of projectively assessed dispositions. Skolnick (1966) reported twenty-year stability coefficients ranging from .21 to .34 for the needs for power, affiliation, aggression, and achievement, although the findings were not consistently replicated across sexes. Britton and Britton (1972) also reported significant stability coefficients for TAT measures of personal and social adjustment over intervals of three, six, and nine years in small samples of men and women aged sixty-five to eighty-five at first testing. The magnitude of these correlations is far smaller than the .60 to .80 which we are accustomed to seeing from self-reports, but that is to be expected. All the literature points to the conclusion that projective tests are relatively poor and unreliable measures of the same dispositions that can be more successfully measured by self-reports. Given the limited reliability of projective tests, the long-term retest correlations from TAT studies can be seen as further evidence of stability.

*   *   *

This chapter set out to consider the criticisms of the stability position that might be offered by personologists with different theoretical and methodological preferences. We conceded that the processes by which behavior is integrated and organized, both moment by moment and over the sweep of a lifetime, are not explicitly addressed by trait models, as they should be in a complete theory of personality. But we also argued that individual differences in these processes, including differences between young and old people, were likely to have trait-like characteristics, and that, in fact, the traits we normally measure are as likely to influence the organization and integration of other traits as they are to influence specific behaviors. To the extent that this is true, we might argue that there are probably no age differences in ego processes.

But is that true? Or are there other organizing features of personality that have eluded the grasp of self-report trait measures? To answer this, we turned to the favored resort of theorists who concentrate on ego processes—projective methods. We found that, to the extent that they depart from the information that could be obtained from self-reports, these measures are generally unreliable and invalid, except perhaps as samples of cognitive behavior or as evidence of shadowy processes (like mastery style) that have little relevance to daily functioning or the course of life. To the extent that they mirror, however dimly, conscious concerns and tendencies, they tend to give evidence of stability in personality.

At this point the astute reader will have noticed that we may have outfoxed ourselves here. We admitted that self-reports might not adequately assess the functioning of the ego and then suggested that we examine projectives. But our assessment of projective techniques hardly leaves us with confidence in any testimony they might offer. Is it not possible, you may ask, that there really are profound changes in the fundamental structure of personality, but that projective tests, with all their limitations, are simply inadequate to the task of finding and documenting them? And if we cannot trust self-reports or projective tests, is there another way to explore the deeper levels of personality? Is there a way to sample the ego at work without letting the ego do the sampling? Is there a way to look for age-related differences in the organization of behavior independent of the trait conceptions embedded in our measures?

Perhaps an objective and trained observer, sensitized to issues of personality organization and allowed to collect whatever information seemed relevant, could accomplish the task. Perhaps what we need is intensive clinical interviews. Many people have thought so, and some of the most important theorizing on adult development has been generated by this method. We will examine it next.

Chapter

6

Adult Development as Seen Through the Personal Interview

The interview is a venerable psychological technique with many variants: the clinical interview is used to gain diagnostic information, the therapeutic interview to help the client think through his or her problems, Levinson's biographical interview to gain a sense of the individual's life, the research interview to gather information. Some interviews, like those conducted by survey researchers and pollsters, are really questionnaires administered verbally rather than in writing; of these we have little to say, since they are essentially self-report instruments. But most interviews involve freer questioning at the discretion of the interviewer, and most require judgments by a rater (who may or may not be the interviewer) rather than simple tabulations of answers. It is these sorts of interviews that we need to consider next, since they have played an important role in theories of adult development.

As a technqiue for gathering information on personality, the interview has a privileged status. Clinicians, who have always dominated personality research and theory, are accustomed to talking directly to patients and to making diagnostic judgments about their condition; it is understandable that they would put particular faith in the results of interviews. The same principles and practices that are used in therapeutic interviews can be applied to normal subjects of pure research.

According to its proponents, the interview has all the advantages of self-report instruments and more. The same questions can be asked by either method, so that the unique experiences of the individuals and their wide knowledge of themselves can be exploited. But in the interview, these self-reports need not be taken at face value.

Perhaps the subject does not seem to understand the question—then it can be rephrased. Perhaps the answers are inconsistent—then the inconsistency can be pointed out or the issue probed more subtly. Perhaps the subject is squirming too much in his or her chair when certain topics are mentioned. The canny interviewer, who is normally a trained professional, can use all these clues to qualify and evaluate the self-reported information. For many researchers the professional interview is the gold standard by which other personality assessments are judged. Farrell and Rosenberg (1981), for example, administered self-report questionnaires to 500 subjects selected to represent the population in general. But most of the conclusions in the book they wrote on their studies are based on interviews with twenty of these men (and their families). The authors simply did not trust the self-reports to give them the complete and unvarnished truth. (As it turned out, the interviews upheld the major conclusions of the self-report study, although many more complexities were uncovered.)

Before deferring completely to the superiority of the interview, however, we should weigh some of its limitations. The results of each interview depend on human judgment, and even expert judgment is fallible. Interviews are typically conducted in one or two hours; at best they may last eight to ten. The interviewer or the rater who interprets the interview must formulate opinions about the person and his or her life on that rather slim basis. What if the subject is nervous and unused to talking about himself? What if he is having an off day? What if the interviewer simply misreads him, thinking that his jokes are intended seriously or that his serious comments are jokes? Is it really wise to try to second-guess the real meaning of an individual's statements?

Even more unsettling is the fact that interview methods are subject to certain kinds of error which are more serious because they are more systematic. If a hundred forty-year-old men are asked how they feel, some will certainly exaggerate how bad things are, and some will surely try to cover up their distress. Some will be having unusually bad days, some unusually good ones. None of the self-reports may be perfectly trustworthy—but *on the average* they are likely to be roughly correct. On the other hand, if one psychologist interviews a hundred men, and if she happens to believe that there is a midlife crisis, she may well accept the stories of the distressed and dismiss the others as defensive distortion. Of course, if she has other biases, she may reach other conclusions equally inconsistent with the facts. The point is that interviewers are not usually impartial observers. Clinicians are trained to see pathology, and see it they will, even in the best-adjusted subjects. Since theorists have a vested interest in finding evidence for the ideas they have advanced, the "data" they find in support of their own ideas must be taken with a certain degree of skepticism.

There are some precautions that can be taken to avoid the introduction of biases. The interviews may be tape-recorded or videotaped, and two or more judges can then rate the subject on the variables of interest. Agreement between them would be evidence that there is some basis in the interview for the inferences that were made and would seem to be a minimum requirement for taking the study seriously. Even perfect agreement, however, would not necessarily mean much. A subject who was extremely nervous during the session might be characterized by both raters as anxious, even though his behavior in the interview was unusual, the result of some temporary and extraordinary circumstance.

Further, an interview is an interpersonal encounter. The interviewer is not an uninvolved, dispassionate observer, but rather an active participant. As any courtroom lawyer will tell you, people can be led to say a great many things under the skillful questioning of an expert. In our courts of law, we try to compensate for this suggestibility by allowing a cross-examination in which a second lawyer, representing an opposite point of view, sees how far the testimony can be shifted in the other direction. In psychological research, this method is never employed (though it might be worth a try). When an adult developmentalist is looking for signs of a midlife crisis in a person, she must act as her own opposing counsel, cross-examining the subject to test all possibilities. Lawyers are not allowed to do this, since they are clearly motivated to help their clients. Researchers, on the other hand, are presumed to be motivated only by a desire for truth.

The pros and cons of the interview method reflect the larger issue that has always profoundly divided personality psychologists: the role of the unconscious. There are those who believe in the unconscious as the real heart of personality, the true source of action, meaning, and value; and there are those who relegate it to a minor role or dismiss it entirely. Communication between these two schools is like an exchange between a believer and an atheist: the fundamental premises are so different that neither can understand why the other thinks as he or she does. Like religion, the unconscious must in part at least be taken on faith. Once its existence and importance are accepted, however, it seems to make sense of many phenomena.

Researchers who prefer interviews are generally believers in the unconscious; they prefer the interpretations of an outside observer because they are fundamentally skeptical of the utility of self-reports. They assume not only that people are unaware of what is really going on in the important parts of their being, but that they are highly motivated to remain unaware, since conflicts, anxieties, and unwelcome impulses predominate in the unconscious. If survey after survey shows no marked increase in depression or anxiety at midlife (Lacy and Hendricks, 1980; Tamir, 1982), this is taken as clear evidence that surveys do not measure the real state of mind.

Researchers who rely on consciousness as the focus of personality are equally skeptical about the claims of interpreters. They point out that hypotheses about the unconscious are often irrefutable: nothing we can do would disprove a dynamic interpretation. If, after several hours of intense probing, an interviewer is unable to find any conflicts that might give evidence of a midlife crisis, she can always conclude that the turmoil and despair are repressed—in fact, this must be an extremely severe crisis, if it was necessary to repress it so thoroughly! Dire predictions of a future crisis are likely to be made, and if anything ever goes wrong in the person's life (as eventually something must), the prediction is trumpeted as proof of the theory.

By now, of course, it must be obvious to readers that our own biases favor conscious over unconscious processes, and self-reports over outside interpretations of personality. On the other hand, we are not prepared to dismiss entirely the contributions of a number of distinguished thinkers who have written extensively on the development of personality in adulthood. In reviewing their positions, we will certainly point out all the reasons we have for disputing many of their conclusions. But we will also try to point out the areas of agreement and the large areas in which their theories and research complement and enrich our own. As we will see, the substance of their findings can often be retained when it is modified or reinterpreted to make it consistent with the facts as we know them. The result, we hope, will be a contribution to the study of emerging lives as well as of enduring dispositions.

Form and Content in Psychological Interviews

As it happens, most of the major theories of adult development are based on interviews rather than on psychological test results. The formulations of Erikson and Gould originated in their clinical practices; the theories of Levinson and his colleagues are based on biographies reconstructed by subject and interviewer. If these researchers have discovered developmental courses standard measures cannot detect, the interview approach may be credited.

In our discussion of the interview method, we have so far been concerned only with the quality of the characterizations it produces. Is Jones an introvert? Do we believe him when he says he is? Or do we observe him during the interview and reach our own decision?

A review of theories of adult development shows, however, that theorists who rely on interviews do not have much to say about extraversion. They are concerned with concepts like the self and the sense of identity; they talk about relationships, roles, life structure. *This difference in substance between interviews and questionnaires is not coincidental. It seems to be a clear instance of form dictating content.*

The typical questionnaire does not let you talk back. The questions must be phrased so that they can be meaningfully answered by all respondents with a choice from yes/no, true/false, or multiple categories (for example, *strongly agree* to *strongly disagree*). If we are interested in job satisfaction, we can ask, "Are you generally satisfied with your job?"; regardless of the kind of job one has, everyone who is employed can answer that question with a simple yes or no. We cannot ask, "What specifically do you like about your job, and what do you dislike?" since the answers to these questions would differ from one job to the next, and standard, precategorized answers would not suffice.

Again, if a questionnaire researcher wants to know how an individual gets along with others, he or she is likely to write a question such as "Do you have many friends?" or "Are you usually dominant in relations to others?" or "Do you believe others are out to get you?" By contrast, an interviewer is likely to say something like "Tell me about your work. How do you get along with your bosses, co-workers, subordinates?" Or "Describe your relationship with your wife and children."

In some respects, we would expect the two methods to yield comparable results. After all, if an individual is really dominant, this should show up in the way he or she deals with friends, co-workers, and family. On the other hand, there are also respects in which important differences may emerge. Questionnaire results are standardized and uniform, independent of the content of the individual's life. Interview results are permeated by the details of an individual's life: the politics at the office or the specific problems of raising a teenage daughter or of living in a declining neighborhood. Case studies with all these details seem to provide a much better feel for the individual's personality than do raw test scores. But what they in fact give is *a better feel for the individual's life structure*, which may or may not be an accurate guide to personality. One's life structure is determined by a thousand forces beyond one's control: economic realities, accidents and illnesses, the help or interference of relatives. These are important elements in understanding the individual's world, but a source of potential confusion in trying to understand the individual.

Interview-Based Theories of Adult Development

At least one of the major theorists we will discuss, Levinson, acknowledges this important difference. He says explicitly that by *adult development* he means the "evolution of the life structure"— although he believes that there is an inner, psychological side to that process that seems akin to personality development. We believe this distinction is crucial to an understanding of the field: nothing we have said about the stability of personality should be interpreted to mean that the life structure does not evolve, and the theories of adult developmentalists need not contradict our position on enduring dispositions. Agreement in principle, however, is not necessarily agreement in practice, and we will have to look at each case closely to see what portion we are willing to believe. We will find, in addition to the distinction between life structure and personality, a second related distinction between self and personality that will also be useful in reconciling differences. That distinction will be explored in the next chapter.

Levinson's Seasons

One of the most influential works on adult development had its major impact before it was published. While still working on his book, *The Seasons of a Man's Life*, Daniel Levinson discussed his ideas with Gail Sheehy, who went on to write the best-selling *Passages*. Levinson's research was based on ten to twenty hours of interviews with forty men in the age range from thirty-five to forty-five. Four occupational groups—executives, workers, biologists, and novelists— were selected to provide some variation, since occupation has a decisive effect on shaping the life course. The subjects were normals; that is, they were not recruited from hospitals or psychiatric clinics, although several had been in psychotherapy at some time in the past.

In the course of the interviews, Levinson and his co-workers began to see a pattern. Instead of finding that the life course was shaped by external events like marriage, job promotions, or illness, they believed they had found evidence of a universal, age-linked series of stages, organized into broader eras. Childhood, Early Adulthood, Middle Adulthood, and Late Adulthood (and possibly Late-Late Adulthood) were the major eras, each lasting about twenty years, and each further was broken into alternating stages of transition and stabilization. The major transitions, including the Mid-Life Transition at age forty to forty-five, overlapped both the preceding and following eras.

The names given to the different stages summarize their developmental meaning. The Early Adult Transition (seventeen to twenty-two) involves breaking away from home and facing adulthood. This stage has already been heavily researched (for example, Constantinople, 1969), since for many individuals it occurs at college, where most subjects for psychological studies are recruited. Entering the Adult World comes next, as the man (the seasons of a woman's life have not yet been charted) begins to function as an adult, usually starting a career and family. These initial attempts at acting like a grown-up are likely to be clumsy, since they begin without the benefit of experience and often with a premature haste to settle down and prove one's adulthood. So between ages twenty-eight and thirty-three the Age Thirty Transition occurs, in which the early occupational and marital choices are reexamined and either rejected, modified, or reaffirmed.

Having made these adjustments, the man enters the period of Settling Down, in which he begins to take life seriously and sets foot on the ladder of success toward his Dream, the ambition he harbors deep down. He is likely in this period to come under the protection, guidance, or sponsorship of a mentor, a somewhat older man whom he admires and who encourages him in his Dream. His wife, also, must do her part to encourage him if he is to be successful. The mentor, who acts somewhat as an older brother, helps the man go from junior adult to senior, but in the latter years of the thirties Becoming One's Own Man becomes crucial, and achievement of occupational aspirations is often accompanied by alienation of the mentor.

Just when life seems to have peaked (at least for those who made it up the ladder), the Mid-Life Transition enters, and everything has to be reevaluated. If men have been successful in striving for their goals, they question whether the goals were meaningful. If they have not been successful, they must reconcile themselves to their failures. In addition, Levinson says, a number of other issues that emerge here must also be dealt with. Men must face the fact that they are getting older, a realization brought about by the beginnings of physical decline and perhaps by the death or disability of their parents. They must also resolve conflicts about masculinity and femininity, creation and destruction, and attachment and separation. In some men these conflicts are expressed as conscious introspection and philosophizing or in artistic creations; in most the conflicts are recognizable only as a sense of turmoil, stagnation, alienation, and confusion.

After age forty-five the individual enters the Mid-Life period with a new basis for living and interpreting life. In the best of cases, concern over personal advancement and proving of one's worth has been replaced by a more altruistic concern for the welfare of others and posterity (Erikson's *generativity*), and the single-mindedness of the thirties is replaced by a new perspective in which previously neglected aspects of the self are given expression.

Although he has not yet made a systematic study of men over age fifty, Levinson assumes that similar stages continue throughout life. The process of *life review* (Butler, 1963), once thought to be a characteristic of old age, may in fact simply be the last of a series of life reviews, undertaken at each transition point throughout life.

Levinson's theory, as he promised, is concerned directly with the life structure and only secondarily with personality. Yet there are two points with important implications for the student of personality. First, to the extent that personality can be identified with values, concerns, and interests, it appears that major changes in personality are being postulated to be the result of aging. Second, the turbulent nature of the life course as described by Levinson suggests that something like change in neuroticism is involved. If individuals go through five-year periods of anguish, conflict, and alienation every few years, measures of psychological distress ought to show it.

This theory is certainly more interesting than the bland assertion that personality is stable in adulthood; the question is, is it true? A careful and critical review of available evidence casts more than a little doubt on the entire scheme. These are among the problems:

Is It Universal? Levinson claims that the sequences he found are universal, at least in his sample. But reading the cases even as he presents them leaves doubts. Some people had ostensibly smooth transition periods; some tried to break out of their life structure when they should have been settling down (of course, they paid the penalty later for that transgression). Among the workers in particular, the success-ladder model did not seem to make much sense: in America there is not much hope for advancement for a thirty-five-year-old factory worker.

Even if it worked in all Americans, the claim for universality seems premature. In support of his claim, Levinson offers the stage theories of Solon, Confucius, and the ancient Hebrews, which he believes show parallels to his theory. But none of these have periods of crisis—surely the cardinal feature of Levinson's scheme—and one is on a ten-year cycle and another on a seven-year cycle. Confucius, for example, says that at age forty he "no longer suffered from perplexities." Does that sound like the beginning of a midlife transition?

What these timetables seem to indicate is a universal recognition that there is growth and activity in the first half of life, and reflection and decline in the second. They also illustrate the universal appeal of dividing up the "seamless web" of adult life into convenient, although essentially arbitrary, stages. The remarkable variety of seemingly natural divisions of the life cycle is clearly shown in an essay on Shakespeare's "seven ages of man" (Chew, 1947).

Is It Intrinsically Age-Related? One of the most controversial features of Levinson's theory is his use of chronological age as the basis for his stages. Most other adult developmentalists prefer to break up the life cycle with marker events like marriage, birth of the first child, and retirement. Sociologically, they argue, the newly wed eighteen-year-old is more like the newly wed twenty-eight-year-old than like his bachelor-age peers. Levinson counters by noting that the marriage of teenagers is likely to be as immature as they are; the event is colored by the period in which it occurs, not vice versa. On the other hand, the teenage father may be immature because he has not had the work and family experience of the twenty-eight-year-old. Experience, not age per se, may be the crucial variable.

Is It Discontinuous? The notion of stages implies qualitative differences between one period and another. Even if the changes that Levinson suggests actually come about, is there evidence that they do so in quantum leaps? Take, for example, the realization that one is growing older. Levinson is probably quite correct in pointing out that the fact of aging requires readjustment. Time goes by continuously, but our conception of ourselves does not change at the same rate. We tend to think we are as we have always been until something confronts us with our age and forces us to acknowledge the change. But it seems unlikely that this occurs in discrete, age-related stages. A thousand incidents may contribute to this insight: a first gray hair, a twentieth anniversary or fortieth birthday, the death of a friend or parent, a newsreel from one's childhood with grotesquely dated fashions and expressions, the observation that college students get younger and more immature each year. Each of these small realizations may be something of a jolt, but is there any evidence that they all occur together, at precisely timed intervals? A man who still thought of himself as a teenager at age thirty-nine probably *would* be in line for a midlife crisis, but are there many men like that?

Is It Personality Change? When Levinson is confronted with evidence of stability in basic personality traits (Rubin, 1981), he tends to dismiss it. Dispositions like anxiety, gregariousness, or aesthetic sensitivity are trivial in his view, superficial aspects of temperament that do not address the real, deep level of personality. For him, the fact that a fifty-year-old man views himself as middle-aged when once he viewed himself as young is a startling change in personality; *young* and *old* are not merely age categories, and calling yourself middle-aged does not mean simply that you are concerned about retirement plans and grandchildren. *Young* and *old* are symbols, Jungian archetypes carrying profound connotations of vitality, immortality, and springtime in contrast with death, decay, and winter. Acknowledgment of middle age is thus a change in the deepest symbolic significance of the self.

Certainly, with age and experience come changes in some aspects of how we view ourselves, and the idea of aging is obviously related at some level to the metaphor of life and death. Perhaps poets are moved by these metaphors to change the style of their poetry as they age. But does the change in the self-concept bring about important changes in the behavior or experience of most individuals? Does it lead them to depression and suicide, or to altruistic self-sacrifice? The answer, we think, is "No." When children leave home, when aged parents require care, when one retires from a lifelong occupation, there are profound changes in the daily routines that constitute the bulk of behavior, but these changes do not amount to changes in personality, and they come about in response to external necessity rather than internal development. Men do not give up playing tennis because they start to feel old; they are more likely to feel old because they have been forced to give up tennis. Nor is there much evidence, as we will soon see, that people feel different during or after one of the transition periods.

Is It Developmental? The field of gerontology has always been fundamentally ambiguous about the *value* of the changes it studies. University departments in this area are typically called "Aging and Human Development," as if the negative connotations of the first word must be offset by more positive ones. Levinson usually writes as if what he is describing were *development*, a positive change, growth, the attainment of higher unity and deeper wisdom. As he progresses through life, the young man learns more about himself and his world and, in the best of cases, is able to rise above the conflicts and illusions of youth to a greater maturity. He can accept the feminine side of his nature, can acknowledge the individuality of his wife; his judgment is improved, marked by realistic compassion rather than by idealism or egocentrism. The older man sees the universal rather than the particular and is no longer bound by shortsighted or parochial views. With the abatement of instinctual drives, the older man can grow in rationality and ego strength. (Of course, Levinson would add, not every man succeeds in development; some despair, some die too young. And the goal is never finally reached: late life, like middle age, is marked by conflict, reassessment, and growth.)

On the other hand, in a discussion of this topic near the end of his book, Levinson expressly denies that his scheme is hierarchical, that later stages are better than earlier ones. Each has its strengths and weaknesses. But while no one stage is intrinsically better than another, the traversing of stages is itself the mark of growth. Individuals who do not change—who experience no periods of crisis— are arrested in development; they are, as a leading theorist of adult development, Orville Brim, says, "stuck" (Rubin, 1981). This view, however appealing and humanistic it seems, has as yet no basis in evidence. Change per se is not necessarily good, nor is stability necessarily the same as stagnation.

Gould's Transformations

If Levinson is fundamentally a Jungian theorist, Gould is clearly a Freudian. He sees adult development as the dismantling of illusions of safety developed in childhood and maintained in a quasiunconscious fashion through the first half of adulthood. His ideas were also borrowed by Sheehy, and he too wrote a book in 1978 expounding his more fully formed theory.

There are both similarities and differences between Gould's and Levinson's work. Gould divides adulthood into five periods: from sixteen to twenty-two, when the adolescent is breaking ties with parents; from twenty-two to twenty-eight, when a new adult life is started; from twenty-eight to thirty-four, when life is reassessed in view of conflicting internal needs and values; from thirty-five to forty-five, when the problems of evil, death, and destruction are faced; and post-midlife, when the individual is finally in control of his or her own destiny. Whereas Levinson calls for alternating periods of stability and transition, Gould sees a continually deepening—and progressively liberating—struggle. Gould expects no further development after fifty, while Levinson does (note that neither of them has studied individuals in this age period). The time frames show some overlap, especially if Levinson's stable periods are ignored, but while Levinson views the timetable as inherent in human nature, Gould believes it is a function of life events and social forces (marriage, birth of children, corporate schedules of advancement). Gould also acknowledges the profound differences of social class. Perhaps the most distinctive feature of Gould's book is his effort to report on women as well as men, and his particular attention to couples.

But the more fundamental differences are to be found in the theoretical underpinnings of *Transformations*. Gould sees the basis for adult development in the unfinished business of childhood. As children we are fundamentally helpless in the face of both outer danger and inner passions of lust, rage, and greed. We depend wholly on our parents to control both these threats, and we internalize a series of false assumptions, illusions that allow us to believe that we are perfectly safe. Maintaining these beliefs has the benefit of preserving our sense of security, but it also has a cost: we are confined by the rules that bound us as children. We cannot get free of these confining inhibitions without facing the illusory nature of some of our most fundamental beliefs and without giving up the security they provide. But when we do get free, we can see reality more clearly and thus stop the rude and unexpected shocks that must repeatedly occur when our illusions collide with life. And, says Gould, we also gain from this process real freedom to be our own persons, in touch with our inner needs and passions, living vital and meaningful lives.

Now, these ideas are by no means novel. Most versions of depth psychology claim that neurotic hangups stem from defenses we adopted in childhood to deal with a reality that no longer exists. Even cognitively based theories of psychotherapy, like Ellis's (1962) Rational-Emotive Therapy, recognize the entrapping and self-perpetuating role of irrational beliefs. Gould's unique contribution is to insist that there is an *age-ordering* of these irrational beliefs. Teenagers entering adulthood confront the assumption that they will always belong to their parents and believe in their world. Achieving independence from parents and their values, taking charge of one's life and one's body, means giving up the comforting assurance that parents will always be there to help and guide.

The young adult who is building a family and beginning a career has joined the establishment—and, says Gould, has done so with a vengeance. The roles of adult, parent, husband, woman, breadwinner are adopted wholesale, in part because the inexperienced adult has no other basis for guidance and in part because he or she believes that following all the rules, working hard, and persevering will guarantee happiness. To be sure, these kinds of activity may well be the best bet for creating a satisfying life, but no behavior can *guarantee* happiness, love, or success, and that is the lesson that must be learned, on an emotional as well as an intellectual level.

By age twenty-eight a new phase starts. The difficulties of building a life tend to have been mastered well enough, and the internal side now clamors for attention. Wishes, values, and feelings that were ignored during the early pragmatic years of getting started suddenly take on a new importance. Career and marriage choices are reevaluated, and we come to the painful conclusion that life is not the simple, controllable affair we imagined. The illusion that we know ourselves and that we are rational, consistent, and independent people is challenged.

Finally, in the midlife decade, an even harder pill must be swallowed: we must admit to ourselves that evil, death, and destruction are a real part of the world and even a real part of us. We have an evil side that may be controlled, but cannot be eliminated; and we face a certain death, with time the only question. The decline of our parents at this time plays a part in shaking the belief that they can save us from ourselves or from external danger. Facing these facts may lead to a period of intense struggle and distress, a midlife crisis. But once the challenge has been confronted, once we have come face to face with our existential aloneness, we achieve the freedom that comes from owning ourselves.

How do we evaluate this theory? As a theory of psychotherapy, its first test would be in its effectiveness in helping clients resolve their problems. In the hands of a skilled clinician like Gould, the theory seems to be effective, but the history of psychotherapy teaches us that, in the hands of a skilled clinician, almost any theory can be effective. More convincingly, research Gould conducted on a large sample of adults who were not patients confirmed that there is a change in the "march of concerns" over the early adult life span: young adults are concerned with getting along with (or away from) their parents, men and women in their twenties are concerned with starting a family and career, complaints of stagnation are more common in the thirties, and facing death and decline is more frequently a problem for those at midlife.

This is important information, although hardly surprising. And a shift in the focus of concerns is something quite different from the evolution of adult consciousness. We might argue, for example, that irrational beliefs would be a dominant feature of the consciousness of only a small minority of individuals—those who require psychiatric treatment. We might grant that all individuals show some of the insights outlined by Gould, but maintain that these changes are trivial readjustments in thinking and not the stuff on which life decisions are made. We might contend that the order of the stages is essentially arbitrary, a result of the most frequent course of events encountered by Americans. A twenty-year-old diagnosed as having cancer may deal with issues of destruction and death before taking on other illusions. If this is the case, *development* seems to be an inappropriate word. Instead, we might view the whole process as one of adaptation to the challenges of living as an adult.

Because Gould's theory is more elastic than Levinson's, it is harder to test. But one of the deductions that can be made from it is that there ought to be notable differences between young and old in basic adjustment and in openness to feelings in particular. Statistically, there is not. In fact, older individuals report being somewhat less open than younger ones, probably because they grew up in a generation that put less value on feelings. A second deduction would be that there are specific periods in adulthood when the struggle with irrational beliefs is particularly strong and overt crisis is likely. For

Gould, this is most likely to be in the midlife period from thirty-five to forty-five. We will consider that possibility next.

In Search of the Midlife Crisis

Of all the features of adult development, the most celebrated is the midlife crisis. Jaques (1965) studied the lives of artists and determined that they all went through a period of crisis precipitated by the recognition of their own mortality. *Time since birth* was replaced by *time left to live* in the mind of the middle-aged man. Peter Chew (1976) wrote a popular account of the crisis, suggesting that marriage stales and the quest for a lost youth leads men to intensified sexual yearnings. Among women, menopause and the loss of children from home were viewed as likely causes of a period of depression and crisis. Levinson (1978) wrote that "for the great majority of men . . . this period evokes tumultuous struggles within the self and the external world" (p. 199) that may appear like neurosis to an outside observer.

These ideas have become so prevalent in both the popular and the scientific press that most people take it for granted that around age forty there is a marked increase in such events as divorce and separation, suicide, job change, and admission to psychiatric hospitals. Epidemiologists who have scrutinized the figures on this issue find very little support for a period of crisis (Kramer and Rednick, 1976). Divorce is most common in the twenties, suicide among the young and the old. Admissions to psychiatric hospitals show no peak at age forty. Still, these are all very rough markers of crisis; perhaps the midlife transition leads to more subtle manifestations.

When Levinson, Gould, and others were first presenting their views on adult development in the early and middle 1970s, the case for stability in personality had not yet been made. The midlife crisis had been pointed out so often that we, like most other psychologists, assumed that it occurred. The major issue, we thought, was to determine its exact timing. Was it between thirty-seven and forty, forty and forty-five? Was the time different for working-class and middle-class men? We used our usual questionnaire methods to try to find an answer. Drawing on the literature describing the characteristics and concerns of men at midlife and the items that Gould (1972) had reported to differentiate patients of different ages, we created a Midlife Crisis Scale and administered it to about 350 men aged thirty to sixty (Cooper, 1977). The scale had items covering sense of meaninglessness, dissatisfaction with job and family, inner turmoil and confusion, and sense of impending physical decline and death.

When we contrasted midlife groups with pre- and post-midlife groups, using various definitions of midlife, we were surprised to find no evidence at all of a peaking of midlife concerns at any age in our range. We had also asked our men to describe in their own words how their lives were going just then. Only seven men (about 2 percent) seemed to fit the category of crisis, and these ranged in age from thirty-four to fifty-six, distributed randomly over the age range we studied. Our conclusion: at any given time, only a small percentage of men are in a crisis, and they are not likely to cluster at any particular age.

Since this conclusion flew in the face of the rest of the literature, our first concern was to replicate it. With a different group of about 300 men, we used a shortened version of the Midlife Crisis Scale. The results were an exact reconfirmation: there was not the slightest evidence of a peaking of distress or midlife characteristics anywhere in the age range we studied (Costa and McCrae, 1978).

Our disenchantment with stages of adult development can be traced to those results, but we are not alone in our reappraisal of the crisis. Farrell and Rosenberg (1981), who had once been proponents of the theory, undertook a major study of the midlife period. We had used the Boston longitudinal study participants for our research, and one criticism that could be raised was that our volunteers were atypical. (Levinson's forty subjects were even less representative of the average man.) Farrell and Rosenberg commissioned a probability sample of about 500 men in the age ranges twenty-five to thirty and thirty-eight to forty-eight, a sample from which generalizations about American men could be made with confidence. They put together a battery of measures of alienation, distress, depression, and crisis, including a midlife crisis scale much like ours in content. They also had measures of what they called *authoritarian denial*, which might be construed as openness versus closedness to experience.

Their analyses, dividing subjects by age and by social class, showed almost exactly what ours had: midlife men were slightly higher in authoritarian denial, but they were actually a bit *lower* in alienation. There was no difference at all on the midlife crisis scale.

But perhaps all these studies make the mistake of tying the crisis to age when stage of life is more important. Among forty-year-old men, some are only recently fathers, many have young children in the home, many others have teenagers, and some have seen all their children grow up and leave home. Perhaps the crisis occurs during one of these stages instead of at a particular chronological age. Indeed, there is evidence from large-scale epidemiological studies

(Tamir, 1982) that men with teenage children are a bit less happy than other men (hardly a surprising finding for those acquainted with teenagers). But most theorists had supposed that the real crisis would come when the children left home, leaving parents to face each other again, with the stark silence reminding them that they were growing old. Some parents do react badly to the departure of their sons and daughters, but in one of the few systematic studies of this stage in the family, Lowenthal and Chiriboga (1972) reported that, if anything, parents were somewhat happier in the empty nest.

"But this proves nothing!" say the critics. "These studies all employed paper-and-pencil tests. What is needed is the insight, probing, and sensitivity of a trained interviewer. He would cut through the facade of well-being and see the crisis brewing just beneath the surface, ready to explode any time into depression, suicide, divorce, alcoholism, dramatic career shifts."

Perhaps. Levinson's interviewers seem to have seen these things. But Farrell and Rosenberg also conducted interviews with twenty of the men they had surveyed, and they came to quite different conclusions. Many men had difficulties in life, but there was no evidence that problems were concentrated at certain periods. Further, the life histories they compiled from several hours of talking with the subjects and their wives and children convinced them that, for the minority who appeared to have a crisis, "the difficulties they experience have their roots in conflicts and problems of earlier origin" and are likely to lead to a "more general process of depressive decline" (p. 215). By contrast, for one who shows most openness and positive adaptation in the middle years, "the sense of self he experiences at midlife is not a marked change from that of early adulthood." In search of a midlife crisis, these researchers emerged from intensive interviews with an impression of stability in the life course.

*   *   *

The interview, it seems, provides more ambiguous accounts of the period of adulthood than do standard personality tests. Some interviewers come to the conclusion that development proceeds in stages; some see no stages at all. There is even greater disparity when the stability of objective test results is contrasted with the growth and development described by interviewers. In part, this is due to the flexibility of the interview as a method of gathering data: if it is more sensitive to the subtle thoughts and feelings of the subject, it is also more sensitive to the biases and preconceptions of the interviewer. In part, however, it is also due to the fact that interviews are typically filled with concrete details from the individual's life, not generalizations about dispositions. Lives surely change, perhaps in stages; personality, we maintain, does not.

We see little basis for adopting the model of development proposed by Levinson and his colleagues, or the more widely held theory of a midlife crisis, and we are skeptical that the processes described by Gould are universal developmental changes in personality or consciousness. But we must admit that the simple statement that personality is stable does not begin to do justice to the full complexity of adult life. The NEO model of personality traits cannot explain the life course, but it may provide some illumination of it. In the next chapter we will try to examine both internal changes of consciousness and external modifications of the life structure as an *interaction* of age and personality. Enduring dispositions may form the scaffolding on which emerging lives are erected.

Chapter
7
The Influences of Personality on the Life Course

Wc havc argucd throughout this book that personality does not change much in adulthood. Our conclusion is based not on theories of development or idealizations of aging, but on a hard look at such facts as we could find. But when we look with equal objectivity at the work of theorists like Levinson and Gould, we cannot escape the conclusion that there is a great deal of change in people's lives. As Gould (1978) writes, "Adulthood is not a plateau." Most people do not begin a career as soon as they leave school and continue in it uneventfully until retirement. Circumstances change, and people change. Part of the resistance to our message of stability comes from the older adult's recognition that life changes and the younger adult's profound hope that there is yet some variety, adventure, and surprise in store. There is.

Perhaps an analogy would help. By the end of high school, or certainly college, most individuals have reached their peak of intellectual development. They are, in a number of demonstrable ways, not only more knowledgeable, but actually more intelligent than they were a few years before. They can think more abstractly, reason more cogently, learn new ideas more quickly, grasp more intricate patterns. At the same time there are enormous differences among twenty-year-olds in intelligence.

Over the course of the life span, we now know pretty well what happens to intelligence. Aside from a slow growth in knowledge (as shown by vocabulary test scores) and a progressive decline in reasoning and perceptual ability, particularly late in life, there is very little change. The average fifty-year-old is about as bright as the average twenty-year-old, and the above-average fifty-year-old is almost certain to have been an above-average twenty-year-old.

But this certainly does not mean that the mind is sunk in stagnation for the greater part of life. Novelists use their intelligence to write books, teachers to educate students, business executives to improve management and expand sales. The work of a lifetime does not lead to *development* of intelligence: a Nobel Prize winner would score no higher on an IQ test after years of research than he or she would have in college. But surely his or her mind has not been wasted. Personality, we submit, is similar in its influence on the adult life. Life does not lead to change or growth in personality, but it allows a fascinating variety of situations in which personal dispositions, for good or ill, play a part.

Some Implications for Personality Theory

We have been concerned throughout this book with the implications of personality research for life-span development, and we will continue that theme in the rest of this chapter. But it is also worthwhile to pause to consider the implications of our developmental findings for personality theory. We have mentioned in passing that the stability of personality traits is important testimony to their reality. If traits were mere fictions or passing fancies, the fleeting reflections of the social pressures of the moment, it would be hard to explain why and how such enduring descriptions of personality could be found.

But our findings speak to the nature of traits as well as to their existence. The widely held belief that personality is the product of childhood experiences, and particularly of styles of child-rearing, does not square well with the repeated finding that there are relatively few and small generational differences in such traits as anxiety, impulsiveness, and openness to feelings. As we discussed in Chapter 2, there have been profound changes in the nature of child-rearing practices in the past fifty years, but their impact on adult personality has been slight.

One interpretation of this finding would be that traits are determined genetically. There is in fact a growing body of evidence that many traits are in part inherited (Buss, 1983; Young et al., 1980). In view of the utility to the species of consistent individual differences, an evolutionary explanation of traits would make sense. Further, genetic theories of personality would certainly be consistent with the stability of personality. But many other theoretical positions could also account for stability, and the evidence to date suggests that a substantial portion of most personality traits *cannot* be explained by genetics.

One of the intriguing problems for personality psychologists is the identification of mechanisms that promote stability. Swann and Hill (1982) have shown experimentally that individuals will actively resist feedback about themselves that is discrepant with their self-conceptions, and self-consistency theorists (Lecky, 1945) have hypothesized that individuals are strongly motivated to maintain a consistent view of themselves. One's associates have the same vested interest in keeping one predictable, so social pressure may also act to preserve the status quo in personality. It seems likely that all these processes and more will be needed to explain the remarkable stability of personality despite changes in social roles, health, and life experiences. Very little else in our world is so dependable.

What Changes?

Let us step back and review for a moment the changes that do occur across the adult portion of the life span. Physically, aging brings with it changes in mobility, sensory capacity, strength, and vigor. Certain cognitive functions, particularly perceptual abilities and memory, show declines, gradually at first, but at an increasing rate as we enter old age. The world also changes as we age (with all the headaches that brings for researchers, as we saw in Chapter 2). Our children grow up and move out, our parents grow old and die. And we are not simply passive victims of the crush of time: we make plans and decisions, change jobs and occasionally spouses. Some of us often and all of us at times think our life is stale and stagnant, but most of us are too busy living to worry about the fact that our personality is not growing.

Leaving aside external influences, we must certainly acknowledge that there are extensive changes in a number of psychological processes. Here are a few:

Behaviors and Habits

Behaviorally oriented psychologists sometimes attempt to define personality as the sum total of all behaviors. Personality psychologists usually laugh at such a definition (if they do not cry), because it represents an incredibly naive attempt to maintain the notion that personality encompasses the whole individual while also reducing it to observable facts. In many circumstances behaviors *reflect* personality, though they also, and much more often, reflect situational demands and constraints and what we have learned by dealing with similar situations. In any case the behavior is not the same thing as the disposition it expresses.

Consequently, there is no contradiction at all in saying that personality remains stable while behavior changes. All this means is that the situation we face in young adulthood, at a certain point in the history of the world, is usually quite different from the situation we face in old age. An active, conventionally masculine individual, for example, is likely to be interested in sports all his life. He will probably participate in team and individual sports in high school and college, but once he takes on a family and career his opportunities for active participation in athletics may be cut drastically, since he no longer has the time or the institutional support. As he moves into middle age, physical limitations may pose yet another obstacle to participation. Professional athletes are normally forced to retire or to become coaches or managers instead of players. Amateurs may change their preferred sport, replacing basketball with tennis or tennis with golf. Physical limitations continue with age, and medical conditions may completely rule out vigorous activity. But an interest in sports and vicarious participation generally continue undiminished: the spirit remains willing, even if the flesh is weakened. And the pace of activity (though not perhaps its vigor) also continues. People who like to keep busy manage to do so in old age by choosing activities that they can handle and perhaps by becoming more efficient in their motions. The range of individual differences even in physical vigor is enormous, and some eighty-year-olds keep up a pace that few twenty-year-olds can match.

Or consider another example. Physicians trained in the 1930s learned to practice a form of medicine that has since been revolutionized several times. Although many of these men and women are still active today, they certainly do not continue to prescribe the same drugs, use the same diagnostic procedures, or perform surgery in the same way. Their interest in medicine and in dealing with patients has continued unabated over the years, but their behavior has changed dramatically. In fact, it is precisely because of their stable commitment to medicine that they have bothered to learn newer developments.

Attitudes and Opinions

The same considerations hold true for ideas, beliefs, and attitudes. Social psychologists devote much of their time to studying the complex and mysterious processes by which attitudes are changed, but we know without doubt that they do change. New develop-ments—like nuclear power and genetic engineering—call for new opinions, and at least some people change their minds on old issues as they continue to think about them. None of this, however, means a change in personality.

Adolescents and young adults are probably more willing than older adults to adopt new values and attitudes or revise old ones (although it is not clear that there is much difference between thirty- and eighty-year-olds). There are two major reasons for this. One is that, as a person ages, really new ideas become increasingly infre-quent, and, as White (1952) remarks, "accumulated experience... more and more outweighs the impact of new events" (p. 333). Another is that, once settled into a life structure, we have much more to lose by changing basic values. The executive rising on the corporate ladder has little incentive to embrace communism; the lawyer who has invested years in learning her profession is under-standably reluctant to question it. Our values, like our personality, help to shape our life structure and are themselves perpetuated by it.

But people do change their minds, just as they change religions, political parties, and occupations. In fact, the enduring personality disposition of openness to experience is in part characterized by the ability to keep an open mind, to consider new opinions, and, at least occasionally, to change attitudes and values. We would expect some people to revise their ideas and values repeatedly, whereas others— the closed—would cling tenaciously to the opinions of their parents and other respected authorities.

Note, however, that change is not necessarily growth. Openness to experience does not guarantee that new opinions and attitudes will always be better—wiser, more differentiated, more in keeping with contemporary reality. Many open people are simply flighty, moving from one world view to another with amazing regularity. When he or she combines openness with critical capacity, however, the open person certainly appears to be in a better position to adapt to a changing world. The point is that change in opinions is not only consistent with stability of personality; it is itself an enduring quality of some individuals.

Social Roles

Few ideas in the social sciences can match the scope or power of the concept of *role*. Social-psychological jargon is full of qualifications of the basic metaphor: role-expectation, role-performance, public role, deviant role, roleless role. Role theorists (Goffman, 1959; Mead,

1934), who tend to be sociologists rather than psychologists, have spent considerable time and effort in proposing and debating various definitions of that eminently useful concept, but for our purposes most of them are equally good. Allport (1961), for example, defined a role as "a structured mode of participation in social life. More simply, it is what society expects of an individual occupying a given position in the group" (p. 181).

Roles are so peculiarly useful because they bridge two of the most crucial of gaps: between the individual and the society and between the self and behavior. Roles are functional units of a social system, and without even referring to individual personality, a sociologist can describe a society by specifying the nature and interaction of roles. A nuclear family, for example, consists of a father and mother (in the complementary roles of husband and wife) and one or more children, who, in addition to being sons and daughters to their parents, are also sisters and brothers to each other. Everyone in this system has a predefined part to play: parents are supposed to take care of the children, but also to control and guide them; children are to love and obey their parents. (The fact that this model family is so seldom seen in reality is a cause for distress to all concerned, but a sophisticated role theorist would point out that the role of teenager in modern America is defined as much by defiance as by obedience.) Other social systems are also understandable in terms of roles: a business consists of bosses, workers, and customers; a city has officials and citizens.

But roles serve an equally important function for individuals, forming the basis for both social definitions and self-definitions. When people are asked to respond to the question, "Who am I?" they are likely to describe themselves by reference to what is called their *social identity*: I am a doctor, a Republican, a mother, a Lutheran. Each person occupies, simultaneously and successively, a dazzling variety of roles, and one of the chief functions of the ego described in Chapter 5 is keeping all of these straight. Much of the individual's sense of identity is tied to the set of roles to which he or she is more or less permanently committed. Nowhere else is the fusion of self and society seen so clearly as in the centrality of role in the definition of both.

For this reason, some psychologists take the view that personality is, or is largely, the collection of roles one plays. To one who maintains such a conception, the contention that personality is stable must seem somewhat silly. Don't people become parents and then grandparents? Don't they retire or make midcareer shifts? Doesn't age increase the probability that one will adopt the sick role? Of course. If one insists on a role theory of personality, the whole issue of stability becomes trivial.

Other psychologists, also influenced by social-role theories, distinguish between roles and underlying personality, but expect that acting out certain roles will lead to changes in personality. The man who takes a job as a policeman may become authoritarian, so the theory goes, because everyone thinks he is and treats him accordingly (Mead, 1934). In laboratory settings, this kind of manipulation can induce changes in people's reports of what they are like.

Our findings of stability present a problem for this theory. Assuming that our measures are taken seriously (and we have spent a good deal of time arguing why they should be), two possibilities emerge as likely explanations. The first is that because role changes are not as pronounced as we might have thought, they leave personality basically unaltered. Perhaps the change from mother to grandmother is not very significant in comparison with differences between fathers and mothers. Again, retirement from an occupation may not be a radical change if, as Havighurst and others have shown (1979), many people continue their professional activities after formal retirement.

A second interpretation is that the role-based theory of personality is simply wrong. Perhaps people do not internalize the perceptions others have of them, laboratory studies notwithstanding. One social psychologist, William Swann, has shown that subjects given feedback inconsistent with their own conceptions of their personality changed their images of themselves—but only until they were given a chance to reassert themselves (Swann and Hill, 1982).

Interpersonal Relationships

Some aspects of interpersonal relationships are based on roles, and as roles change, so do relationships. Soldiers who fought on opposite sides can be friends when the war is over; students become the colleagues of their professors when they graduate; retired executives can no longer dominate others as they used to. These changes in relationships are perhaps the most significant feature of changes in roles.

Other aspects of interpersonal behavior are expressions of traits that cut across many different roles and impart a personal flavor to their interpretation. As far as role requirements allow, the friendly person is likely to respond with warmth to employers, neighbors, and relatives. The shy person will be self-conscious among strangers, but also with friends when he or she is too much the center of attention. Because these dispositions cut across roles, the changes in roles that come with age do not affect their expression, and they tend to remain stable across the adult years.

But there are some relationships that are shaped by more than social-role requirements or personal dispositions. Farrell and Rosenberg (1981), for example, in their discussion of husbands and wives at midlife acknowledge that the adage that opposites attract has rarely been supported by research, but point out that couples seem to develop a pattern of complementary behavior. Two assertive individuals may make a couple in which one is clearly dominant, or they may carve out separate domains in which to exercise their dominance: traditionally, the wife ran the house and the husband made decisions about the car. Whenever two individuals share a significant and lasting relationship, its characteristics are likely to be the result of the particular ecology of both persons and the situation, a series of compromises and adaptations evolved over a period of time.

Psychoanalytically oriented theorists will insist that significant adult relationships always echo in some form the earlier patterns of the child's interactions with his or her parents, and perhaps they are right. Certainly trait theory by itself is not a sufficient basis for understanding the complexities of an adult relationship. Dependency is one of the perennial sources of conflict in marriages, for example, and it figures prominently in the problems that individuals bring to therapy. Yet few trait systems contain well-validated measures of this construct. Dependency may exist only as a feature in human relationships, never as a trait characterizing a single individual.

We might describe a relationship as the patterns of power and dependency, the emotional support given or received, the depth and nature of the bond of love or hatred. Little is known about the stability of these features of relationships. Do newlyweds quickly set up a pattern that will endure throughout married life, or are the terms constantly renegotiated as new problems and opportunities—the birth of a child, a career for the wife, an older parent moving in— emerge? Is it possible that there are regular developmental changes that characterize relationships, not individuals? Do wives take over the decision-making roles in the family after middle age, even though they do not otherwise become more assertive or masculine?

One set of relationships does show change closely related to age. As we age, we become independent of our parents and our children become independent of us. Interview studies seem unanimously to suggest that the intrapsychic rate of change by no means keeps pace with the behavioral. Years after moving away from home and taking financial responsibility for themselves, adults often seem curiously tied to the approval and opinions of their parents. Some writers argue that it is only the shock of a parent's death or chronic disability that convinces middle-aged men or women that they are really as big and strong as their parents once were. The struggles of the adolescent to break away from parental domination sometimes result in periods of many years in which there seems to be no feeling at all left for parents. Levinson's interviews suggest that at middle age the feelings, positive and negative, may reawaken and lead to a new, perhaps more mature relationship.

It is of some interest to note that studies of the external trappings of family life show great continuity between generations (Troll, Miller, and Atchley, 1979). The majority of adult children see their parents at least once a week, and considerable mutual support is offered in the form of money, favors, and so on. These family ties generally continue until death; the notion that most old people are abandoned by their children is largely myth.

Identity and the Self

Having considered separately values, roles, and relationships, we are in a position to talk about the self and its development in adulthood. But we are immediately faced with another of the problems in terminology that plague psychology: there are no generally agreed upon definitions of the self. We will offer some distinctions that can at least be useful here.

We will use the term *self* to refer to the entire person from a psychological perspective. Correspondingly, the *self-concept* is the individual's view of his or her self. Every assertion one might agree to in the form of "I am ... " describes an aspect of the self. As Rosenberg (1979) explains, the contents of the self-concept include social roles, intimate relationships, body image, and self-ideal, as well as abilities and dispositions. What we have been calling *personality*— enduring dispositions in the domains of neuroticism, extraversion, and openness to experience, as well as traits like masculinity and conscientiousness—thus forms only one part of the self, although certainly a major part. Our finding of stability in this part of the self does not imply that other parts of the self do not change.

Our use of the words *self* and *personality* is almost the opposite of that adopted by a noted developmentalist, Douglas Kimmel (1974). Kimmel uses the term *personality* to represent the entire psycho-social system and restricts the self to its central core. He concurs in our finding that personality traits are generally stable, whereas social behavior and roles (which he considers less central) change with age. He expresses this, however, by saying that some aspects of personality are more stable, some less stable. We agree in substance, but would rephrase his formulation to say that personality is one aspect of the self that is stable in adulthood.

Kimmel's usage does draw attention to the fact that some parts of the self seem to be more meaningful and consequential than others.

We would recommend the word *identity* to refer to those aspects of the self that are essential to one's self-definition. Personality traits may be a salient part of one's identity, but so may social definitions or body image. Whether and in what ways identity changes in adulthood is only beginning to be explored. Whitbourne and Waterman (1979) have traced the development of identity from college age (by which time Erikson suggested it should be formed) through the thirties and report an increase in commitment over this period—a conclusion that echoes White's (1952) finding of "stabilization of ego identity" in his case studies covering a similar period of development. Does identity continue to stabilize, or are the identity crises of adolescence revived at middle age? Is the process more gradual but no less inexorable? Whitbourne is currently examining identity in older individuals, and a review of the development of the self is also offered by Breytspraak (in press).

One aspect of the self has been studied extensively: self-evaluations. *Self-esteem* is measured as often as any other personality variable, in part because it has commanded the attention of sociologists and in part because it has seemed to be central to many self-based theories of personality and psychopathology. Our research suggests that poor self-esteem is heavily influenced by neuroticism, especially depression and vulnerability, and that positive self-esteem, or self-confidence, is related to extraversion. We would thus expect stability in measures of self-esteem, and the literature to date sustains our conclusions (Mortimer, Finch, and Kumka, 1981). As they age, people may come to feel that their social identity is less important than their personal characteristics or that their identity as a daughter or son has changed with the death of their parents. But regardless of how they see themselves, or how the view changes, extraverts are likely to be pleased, neurotics unhappy, with what they see.

Shaping the Life Course

Is that the best we can do—admit that some aspects of the person and his or her world change with age, even though personality does not? Is this really the end of the study of aging and personality?

We do not think so; in fact, we would say that it is more like the beginning. Ideally at this point we would review an extensive literature showing the many ways in which personality not only endures, but actively shapes adult life. We would describe the typical career paths of extraverts, the marital history of introverts, the ways in which open people adapt to aging and disease. Unfortunately, there is as yet little to review. Students of age and personality have always asked, "How does aging change personality?" rather than "How does personality change aging?" Some research, generally undertaken for quite different reasons, can be cited as a sample of the kind of findings we may someday have. For now, however, we must be content with the few studies that have been done, with speculation, and with suggestions for the kind of research that could be done.

As we noted in Chapter 4, in order to make a life for oneself at all one must have some firm foundations, some predictable regularities. Some sources of continuity are external to us, including our cultural background and social class, and socialization into particular professions or groups. We remain much the same in our talents and abilities, and, although we face uniform declines in health and vigor, the changes tend to be gradual.

The same considerations apply to personality dispositions. Choosing a major in college, deciding whom to marry, accepting a job transfer, planning for retirement—all depend on the knowledge that our basic motives and styles will endure. Bandura (1982) argues that part of the reason for stability in personality may be that we choose and create environments that will reinforce our dispositions; regardless of the reasons, stability is a fact we must and do count upon.

Psychological Adjustment across the Life Span

One of the sorriest truths that has emerged from the experience of psychologists in the last century is that individuals with difficulties in living generally continue to have problems, even after extensive treatment. Tsuang and colleagues (1981) have shown that 92 percent of individuals diagnosed as schizophrenic thirty years ago are still judged schizophrenic today. Twenty-five years after World War II, Keehn and his colleagues (1974) found that soldiers given psychiatric discharges were more likely to have died from suicide, homicide, accidents, or alcohol-related illnesses than normal soldiers with the same war experiences. Robins (1966) showed that deviant children are much more likely than others to become adult criminals, and recidivism rates from police records show that an adult criminal generally leads an entire lifetime of crime. But schizophrenia is an illness, and the social system may trap some individuals into a pattern of crime. Do enduring personality traits in normal individuals affect long-term adjustment to life?

Certainly. Neuroticism is the aspect of personality most relevant to adjustment, and those high on this dimension are likely to show evidence of maladjustment at all ages. They are, for example, likely to be dissatisfied with life and low in measures of recent mood (Costa and McCrae, 1980a). Maas and Kuypers (1974) found in a forty-year follow-up study of a group of men that "old age does not usher in or introduce decremental psychological processes. Rather, old age may demonstrate, in perhaps exacerbated form, problems that have long-term antecedents" (p. 203). There is evidence that, regardless of age, individuals high in neuroticism are more likely to use ineffective coping mechanisms like hostile reactions, passivity, wishful thinking, and self-blame in dealing with stress. Vaillant (1977) has documented the pervasive influence of neurotic coping styles on the lives of an elite group, Harvard graduates.

But this is nothing new; it is merely a restatement of the fact that neuroticism is an enduring and consequential disposition. It is in interaction with age and time that the influence of neuroticism becomes most intriguing. Consider, for example, individuals who experience a so-called midlife crisis. Everyone acknowledges that there are such people, although there is dispute as to how many. The problems and concerns of this syndrome are distinct: they revolve around the themes of lost youth, abandoned dreams, meaningless relationships. When Farrell and Rosenberg (1981) interviewed five subjects who seemed to be in this state, they concluded from detailed life histories that this was not simply a "developmental emergent" without precedent in the life of the individual. Even if the individual had led a relatively solid and satisfying life up to that point, these researchers believed that the seeds of crisis had already been laid by defects in his character and the resulting poor choices he had made.

We found evidence of another sort for the same phenomenon. In our questionnaire studies of the midlife crisis (described in Chapter 6), we found that only a minority of men of any age felt themselves to be in a crisis. When, however, we examined the scores these few had received on personality measures taken ten years earlier, we found that even then they had been significantly higher in neuroticism. If we spoke to these men today, we might find them blaming all their troubles on recent events or on their age or health. But they had had more than their share of complaints many years earlier, and it begins to seem that they carried their troubles with them. It may be that it is the *form* of the trouble that varies with the period of life in which they happen to be. Gould (1972) found that the nature of the concerns that brought patients to therapy differed by age: adolescents had problems with their parents, young adults with career choices. Well-adjusted individuals who go through the same situations regard them as challenges rather than insoluble problems.

A somewhat different interaction is seen in recent work by Liker and Elder (in press). They set out to explore the joint impact of an environmental event (downward economic mobility caused by the Great Depression) and the disposition of neuroticism on a significant life outcome: the quality of marital relations. They found a number of interesting things in a design that included several measurements over a period of years. The emotional stability of both partners had a continuing impact on the quality of their marriage, although the quality of their marriage had no influence on their personality. Economic depression seemed to have a psychologically depressing effect on some individuals, since the general level of adjustment declined a bit.

Most interesting to us, however, was the *differential* effect of financial loss. Initially well-adjusted men tended to bounce back, while those who were neurotic to begin with became more so under stress: "Depression losses affected the temperament of irritable men more than three times as much as the temperament of relatively calm men.... Economic pressure accentuated personality tendencies harmful to marriage."

Such studies as these point the way to whole new lines of research, since they show that neither our dispositions in themselves nor the circumstances that age and history confront us with are sufficient to explain the forms (or failures) of our adjustment. Instead of being content to ask, "How do older people adjust to retirement or bereavement or relocation?" we may find that we have to ask, "How do older neurotic people...?" or "How do older open extra-verts...?" We can be reasonably confident that those high in neuroticism will handle a change badly, but even this may not be the case: Lieberman (1975) has shown that it may be adaptive for older persons to be irritable and demanding when in a nursing home, because it may get them necessary attention. The enduring disposition that caused nothing but trouble for seventy years may lead to longer life at the end.

Making Life Choices

Much of the conduct of life is routine: going to work, doing errands, cleaning the house, watching television. However humdrum they may seem, these routines are generally the result of an elaborate evolution intended to allow us to gratify most of our needs most of the time as well as we can in our circumstances. What seems unremarkable from its familiarity is in fact an intricate construction, a life structure. As we continue to age, a succession of life structures forms a life course, and we have from time to time the opportunity to modify it by making critical choices.

Critical choices, and the reasons behind them, form the substance of biographies (Herold, 1963): Napoleon decides to restore order to the French Revolution, in part because of his conservative social views; he has himself crowned emperor to satisfy his quest for personal aggrandizement; he divorces Josephine and marries Maria Louisa to ensure the rights of his progeny; he invades Russia because he believes he can bully Alexander into submission; he returns from Elba because he has become convinced that, despite all odds, it is his destiny. Biographers generally feel that the best way to understand the individual's personality is to record their subject's life, to analyze the circumstances that helped shape the life course (in part to separate external influences from the inner characteristics), and then to interpret the action in terms of the inner drives, talents, or weaknesses of the person (Runyan, 1981). Erikson (1962) has devoted much of his career to such psychobiographies, and most clinicians rely heavily on the life history as a means of understanding their clients. (Since clinicians rarely have the historian's grasp of the surrounding circumstances, they may be inclined to exaggerate and overinterpret the role of the individual in shaping—or misshaping—his or her life.)

Empirically oriented psychologists have always felt uncomfortable with these case studies and with good reason: various explanations can usually be offered for the same facts, and there is no conclusive way to choose among them. Different historians have vastly different views of the character of Napoleon and make widely different hypotheses about what he would have done if Wellington had left him any choice. But we cannot conduct an experiment, cannot go back in time and manipulate history so as to test these theories. And, according to most philosophers of science, what is untestable is beyond the bounds of science.

Still, the principle is too appealing to give up: surely people's lives do reflect their nature, and surely personality shapes people's lives. If we are interested in people in general, rather than in some particular historical figure, we can move from speculative biography to testable psychology. We can also abandon the post hoc method of looking for traits that underlie life choices and begin a systematic study of the effects of specified traits on individual lives. We are not all Napoleons, but we do make choices: if and when and whom to marry; whether to have children and how many; what career to pursue, when to change it, when to persist despite adversity; whether to move to another city and reestablish friends and routines.

Somewhat surprisingly, there has been relatively little research on shaping the life course, although some of the major decisions have been examined separately. Curiously, the two most significant and most thoroughly researched life choices—marriage and career—show quite different patterns.

Marriage

Theories of marital choice have generally looked for a basis in either similarity or complementarity. There is good evidence that people do marry others of similar social, ethnic, and religious backgrounds, and that physical attractiveness is a powerful determinant—the rich and beautiful tend to marry the rich and beautiful. There is also clinical evidence, of the kind reported by Farrell and Rosenberg, that marital relationships often evolve complementary functions. But when personality measures are used, they uniformly fail to predict marital choice. Extraverts are just as likely to marry extraverts as introverts; adjusted people choose neurotic spouses as often as adjusted spouses. There seems to be a small influence of similarity in the domain of openness—open people tend a bit toward marrying open people—but that may be due to similarities in social class, education, and so on. When two college graduates marry, both of them are likely to be more open than high school dropouts.

This might seem to be a defeat for trait psychologies: the major dimensions of individual difference seem to have little influence on one of the most significant decisions of our life. Indeed, it is a healthy reminder that traits cannot explain *everything*. But it leads to a series of fascinating and thus far almost completely unexplored questions. Why would a well-adjusted person take on the difficult task of trying to live with an anxious, hostile, and depressed mate? Why would an open person consent to life with one who was closed? And, more than why, *how* do they manage together? When an introvert marries an extravert, does it lead to conflicts in their joint social life, or do they arrange to live separate lives, or does the extravert bring out the extraverted side of his or her spouse? Does it matter whether the husband or the wife is the introvert: will the husband's preferred style of socializing prevail regardless of what it is? Psychologists have spent a great deal of time studying how one individual adapts to an environment, but how do two individuals adapt to the environment they create for each other?

Careers

On the second issue, career choice, the influence of personality is both better understood and more obvious. Given a choice, people tend toward occupations that allow the expression of their personality. This is most clearly seen in inventories of vocational interest, like the Holland (1977) Self-Directed Search, which provides scores for six categories of interests. Individuals with enterprising and social vocational interests tend to be extraverts; those with artistic interests tend to be open. Investigative interests are found among intelligent introverts, realistic interests among masculine men and women, and conventional interests among those closed to experience. Not surprisingly, open people report interest in a wider variety of occupations of all sorts.

Similar relations are found when other vocational interest inventories, with different categorizations of interests, are used. And after age twenty-five, vocational interests are known to be extremely stable. Until the past five years, the best evidence for stability in personality was that provided by Strong's (1955) twenty-five-year retest of vocational interests.

When we move from vocational interests to actual occupation, the data become less clear. Open people may be interested in the occupation of poet or concert pianist, but how many of them have the talent or the financial resources to make a career of these interests? At this point in history at least, one's gender and educational level are the primary determinants of occupational choice and economics is the major incentive. By and large, people take the highest-paying job they are qualified for, regardless of their preferences. Given a choice, they will gravitate toward the positions best fitted to their temperament—but most of us are not really given a choice. Nevertheless, studies do show that salespeople are more likely to be extraverts than introverts and that cooks are less open to experience than are creative writers (Cattell, Eber, and Tatsuoka, 1970).

Once one has taken a job, for whatever reason, personality is likely to manifest itself in the way the job is performed. The extraverted bank clerk will spend more time than others chatting with customers; the librarian closed to experience may make more efforts to maintain quiet than to encourage reading. And if the gap between the occupational demands and personal dispositions is too large, the individual is likely to quit and find a different line of work.

We know from studies in Boston (Costa and McCrae, 1978) and in Baltimore that individuals who have started a new career or switched to a different line of work are much more likely to be open than closed to experience. This is as true for women as it is for men. Longitudinal studies have also allowed us to separate cause from effect: people are not open *because* they were broadened by a new vocational experience; instead, they were open to experience years before they made the change, and it seems likely that openness contributed to the decision to start a new career.

Like most researchers, we have been concerned primarily with changes that overtake the individual, and failed to consider the changes that come as the individual overtakes his or her own life. One of the chief merits of the studies of Levinson, Gould, and others is that they remind us that problems can result when life fails to change. We strive to succeed in our careers and must cope with failure, but we must also deal with success. What motivation remains for the Nobel laureate who has won the prize that inspired his or her life's work? What happens to the couple whose dream of a house in the suburbs is finally realized? People soon come to take for granted the achievements that once dominated their lives. What happens then—depression, new dreams, rededication to the same cause? And what is the role of personality in this process?

Personality Influences on the Development of Identity

We have tried to distinguish between personality traits, the self, and identity, noting that personality forms one unchanging aspect of the self, whereas identity consists of the most central aspects of the self (self-definitions in terms of roles, relationships, and values, as well as personal characteristics) and may or may not change. Since traits and identity elements are usually mixed indiscriminately under the label *personality* or *self-concept*, few researchers have thought to ask whether traits influence the development of identity. The question, however, is intriguing.

It is useful to begin by recalling that there is no one-to-one correspondence between the roles one plays in society and the definitions one has of oneself. The fact that one works from 9:00 to 5:00 as a secretary does not mean that being a secretary is part of one's self-definition. In fact, many secretaries probably see themselves as housewives, novelists, or doctors who are merely taking a job as a secretary; their dreams and aspirations are elsewhere. Conversely, even when we fill a role that we have always hoped to fill, we may not really believe we fit in. In the eyes of the law, we may be fully adult at age eighteen or twenty-one; in our own eyes it may take many more years. In the meantime we act as adult as possible and hope that others will believe our bluff. Symbols are often important in establishing our sense of identification with a role. Stethoscopes may be more important than licenses in making men and women feel like doctors; military and religious uniforms are indispensable in creating the sense of commitment and identification that is required by these institutions.

A number of clinicians have remarked on the discrepancies between the face we present to the world—our persona or mask, as

Jung called it—and our real sense of self. Alienation and a sense of meaninglessness may result from acting out roles with which we cannot identify. Conversely, we may identify too closely with superficial roles, at the risk of being at best shallow, at worst seriously out of touch with our own inner needs.

It seems likely that openness to experience would figure importantly in the correspondence between inner and outer versions of the self. Those who are open to their own feelings, willing to think out and try out new ways of living, should develop a better fit in the long run. There is a bit of empirical support for this hypothesis in a study of organizational behavior conducted by Kahn and his associates (1964). They employed the California Personality Inventory to measure a trait called *flexibility-rigidity*, apparently a close cousin of openness. Said Kahn, "The strong identification with his superiors and with the official goals of the organization, together with the heavy emphasis on authority relations, leads the rigid person to a rather complete internalization of his roles. His role tends to become his identity. While the flexible person may be in the course of the work day a manager, friend, personal confidant, sports fan, and explorer, the rigid person is *manager*" (p. 294). What becomes of such a person when he retires? Is he now *retired*, content to be nothing more productive? Or does he face a crisis in the loss of an identity in which he was too heavily invested? Is the departure of children from the home more stressful for the closed woman who has always regarded herself as nothing but *mother*? Surely these transitions must have different impacts on open and closed people.

Theorists have often noted the importance of fantasy in the acquisition of new roles. Imagining oneself as a senator, making speeches and debating foreign policy, may be important as a first step in running for election—even to a much lesser office. The housewife's ability to see herself with an independent career probably smooths the way for her when she begins looking for a job or returns to school. A certain flexibility in self-concept as well as a degree of openness would thus appear to contribute to change.

The same considerations may apply to relationships as to roles. We know that closed persons espouse traditional family ideologies (Costa and McCrae, 1978); they may also be the kinds of people who preserve a single style of relating to significant others throughout their lives. For them, perhaps, father and mother remain the only real adults, to be loved or feared, but never recognized as people with their own limitations. For them, perhaps, wives remain homemakers and husbands breadwinners, and woe to a spouse who fails to live up to these expectations or tries to exceed them! For them, perhaps, children never grow up and are always to be advised or scolded or praised according to how well they live up to parental standards.

Gould's work on adult development is concerned with the achievement of adult consciousness: the profound realization that we control our own lives and must take responsibility for them; that life is not necessarily fair and railing against injustice will not make it so; that we ourselves are not innocents, but have a darker side; that death will come to us as to our parents. Gould sees these insights emerging over the first half of life in a regular sequence. But are they universal? Or is it perhaps only the open individual who sees and feels enough of life to make these discoveries and reach the real freedom that freedom from illusion allows?

*   *   *

The last few years have been extraordinarily productive ones for the field of personality and aging. Longitudinal studies begun years ago by farsighted researchers have offered clear and consistent evidence of what happens to personality dispositions with age. In the same period personality psychology itself has revived from a period of skepticism and stagnation, bringing new vitality to an area that has proved itself indispensable in helping us to understand human beings and their lives. We have made conceptual advances and have come to see that much of what we were quarreling about was words instead of facts. A good deal has now been established, and a completely new direction for research on personality and aging can now be envisioned.

Personality has often been identified with the organizing force in human behavior, and more systematic studies of the processes of organization are still necessary. But personality can also be viewed as the product of organization, the sum of recurring regularities that mark the style of each person and distinguish him or her from others. We call these individual consistencies *traits*.

Despite the many systems and labels, some common ground has been reached in identifying the most important groups of traits. Neuroticism and extraversion are nearly unanimous choices; openness to experience is gaining increasing recognition. We know that we can measure these traits with an acceptable degree of accuracy by either self-reports or ratings from knowledgeable sources.

We have learned all the pitfalls of assuming that cross-sectional comparisons show age changes, and have considered the evidence from longitudinal and sequential designs as well. And study after study has shown that over the adult portion of the life course there is little change in the average level of the commonly measured personality traits. In general there is neither growth nor decline in adult personality. A psychology whose purpose was to explain how personality changes with age would have nothing to say. Indeed, it becomes more pertinent to explain how personality remains stable.

For stable it is, not only in groups, but in individuals. Longitudinal studies using a variety of instruments, and using raters as well as individuals' own reports, find great continuity in the level of traits in individuals. These same findings are confirmed by retrospective accounts that show the same traits active in youth and in old age.

But the stability of traits does not imply that life itself must be repetitious and stagnant. Lives change, history moves on, and all of us must work to adapt to change, or actively reshape our lives. Internally, our sense of self, our fundamental identity, may change as the social roles, values, physical attributes, and personal relationships that are central to it shift.

It is in the study of these changes that the future of personality and aging lies. Ask not how life's experiences change personality; ask instead how personality shapes lives and gives order, continuity, and predictability to the life course, as well as creating or accommodating change. For the psychologist as well as the aging individual, enduring dispositions form a basis for understanding and guiding emerging lives.

References

Allport, G. W. *Personality: A psychological interpretation*. New York: Holt, 1937.

Allport, G. W. *Becoming: Basic considerations for a psychology of personality*. New Haven: Yale University Press, 1955.

Allport, G. W. *Pattern and growth in personality*. New York: Holt, Rinehart and Winston, 1961.

Allport, G. W. Traits revisited. *American Psychologist*, 1966, *21*, 1–10.

Allport, G. W., and Odbert, H. S. Trait names: A psycho-lexical study. *Psychological Monographs*, 1936, *47*, No. 211, 1–171.

Ames, L. B. Changes in the experience balance scores on the Rorschach at different ages in the life span. *Journal of Genetic Psychology*, 1965, *106*, 279–286.

Arenberg, D., and Robertson-Tchabo, E. A. Learning and memory. In J. E. Birren and K. W. Schaie (Eds.), *Handbook of the psychology of aging*. New York: Van Nostrand Reinhold, 1977.

Atkinson, J. W., Bongort, K., and Price, L. H. Explorations using computer simulation to comprehend thematic apperceptive measurement of motivation. *Motivation and Emotion*, 1977, *1*, 1–27.

Bachman, J. G., O'Malley, P. M., and Johnston, J. *Adolescence to adulthood: Change and stability in the lives of young men*. Ann Arbor, MI: Institute for Social Research, 1978.

Baltes, P. B., and Nesselroade, J. R. Cultural change and adolescent personality development. *Developmental Psychology*, 1972, *7*, 244–256.

Baltes, P. B., Reese, H. W., and Nesselroade, J. R. *Life-span developmental psychology: Introduction to research methods*. Monterey, CA: Brooks/Cole, 1977.

Bandura, A. *Social learning theory*. Englewood Cliffs, NJ: Prentice-Hall, 1977.

Bandura, A. The psychology of chance encounters and life paths. *American Psychologist*, 1982, *37*, 747–755.

Barron, F. The ego-strength scale and its correlates. In W. G. Dahlstrom and L. Dahlstrom (Eds.), *Basic readings on the MMPI: A new selection on personality measurement*. Minneapolis: University of Minnesota Press, 1980.

Berg, I. A. The unimportance of test item content. In B. M. Bass and I. A. Berg (Eds.), *Objective approaches to personality assessment*. New York: Van Nostrand, 1959.

Block, J. *The Q-sort method in personality assessment and psychiatric research*. Springfield, IL: Charles C Thomas, 1961.

Block, J. *The challenge of response sets*. New York: Appleton-Century-Crofts, 1965.

Block, J. *Lives through time*. Berkeley, CA: Bancroft Books, 1971.

Block, J. Some enduring and consequential structures of personality. In A. I. Rabin (Ed.), *Further explorations in personality*. New York: Wiley-Interscience, 1981.

Block, J. H., and Block, J. The role of ego-control and ego-resiliency in the organization of behavior. In W. A. Collins (Ed.), *Development of cognition, affect, and social relations: The Minnesota symposium on child psychology*, Vol. 13. Hillsdale, NJ: Lawrence Erlbaum, 1980.

Breytspraak, L. M. *The development of self in later life*. Boston: Little, Brown, in press.

Britton, J. H., and Britton, J. O. *Personality changes in aging: A longitudinal study of community residents*. New York: Springer, 1972.

Bühler, C. The curve of life as studies in biographies. *Journal of Applied Psychology*, 1935, *19*, 405–409.

Bühler, C., Keith-Spiegel, P., and Thomas, K. Developmental psychology. In B. B. Wolman (Ed.), *Handbook of general psychology*. Englewood Cliffs, NJ: Prentice-Hall, 1973.

Buss, D. M. Evolutionary biology and personality psychology: Implications of genetic variability. *Personality and Individual Differences*, 1983, *4*, 51–63.

Butler, R. N. The life review: An interpretation of reminiscence in the aged. *Psychiatry*, 1963, *26*, 65–76.

Caldwell, B. McD. The use of the Rorschach in personality research with the aged. *Journal of Gerontology*, 1954, *9*, 316–323.

Cattell, R. B. *Personality: A systematic theoretical and factual study*. New York: McGraw-Hill, 1950.

Cattell, R. B., Eber, H. W., and Tatsuoka, M. M. *The handbook for the Sixteen Personality Factor Questionnaire*. Champaign, IL: Institute for Personality and Ability Testing, 1970.

Chew, P. *The inner world of the middle-aged man*. New York: Macmillan, 1976.

Chew, S. C. "This strange eventful history." Paper presented at the Folger Shakespeare Library, Washington, DC, April 23, 1947.

Coan, R. W. Measurable components of openness to experience. *Journal of Consulting and Clinical Psychology*, 1972, *39*, 346.

Cohen, J. *Statistical power analysis for the behavioral sciences*. New York: Academic Press, 1969.

Constantinople, A. An Eriksonian measure of personality development in college students. *Developmental Psychology*, 1969, *1*, 357–372.

Cooper, M. W. An empirical investigation of the male midlife period: A descriptive, cohort study. Unpublished undergraduate honors thesis, University of Massachusetts at Boston, 1977.

Costa, P. T., Jr., Fozard, J. L., and McCrae, R. R. Personological interpretation of factors from the Strong Vocational Interest Blank scales. *Journal of Vocational Behavior*, 1977, *10*, 231–243.

Costa, P. T., Jr., and McCrae, R. R. Age differences in personality structure: A cluster analytic approach. *Journal of Gerontology*, 1976, *31*, 564–570.

Costa, P. T., Jr., and McCrae, R. R. Age differences in personality structure revisited: Studies in validity, stability, and change. *Aging and Human Development*, 1977, *8*, 261–275.

Costa, P. T., Jr., and McCrae, R. R. Objective personality assessment. In M. Storandt, I. C. Siegler, and M. F. Elias (Eds.), *The clinical psychology of aging*. New York: Plenum Press, 1978.

Costa, P. T., Jr., and McCrae, R. R. Influence of extraversion and neuroticism on subjective well-being: Happy and unhappy people. *Journal of Personality and Social Psychology*, 1980, *38*, 668–678. (a)

Costa, P. T., Jr., and McCrae, R. R. Still stable after all these years: Personality as a key to some issues in adulthood and old age. In P. B. Baltes and O. G. Brim (Eds.), *Life-span development and behavior*, Vol. III. New York: Academic Press, 1980. (b)

Costa, P. T., Jr., and McCrae, R. R. An approach to the attribution of age, period, and cohort effects. *Psychological Bulletin*, 1982, *92*, 238–250.

Costa, P. T., Jr., McCrae, R. R., and Arenberg, D. Enduring dispositions in adult males. *Journal of Personality and Social Psychology*, 1980, *38*, 793–800.

Costa, P. T., Jr., McCrae, R. R., and Arenberg, D. Recent research on personality and aging. In K. W. Schaie (Ed.), *Longitudinal studies of adult development*. New York: Guilford Press, 1983.

Dollard, J., and Miller, N. E. *Personality and psychotherapy: An analysis in terms of learning, thinking, and culture*. New York: McGraw-Hill, 1950.

Douglas, K., and Arenberg, D. Age changes, cohort differences, and cultural change on the Guilford-Zimmerman Temperament Survey. *Journal of Gerontology*, 1978, *33*, 737–747.

Edwards, A. L. *Statistical methods for the behavioral sciences*. New York: Holt, Rinehart and Winston, 1954.

Edwards, A. L. *The social desirability variable in personality assessment and research*. New York: Dryden, 1957.

Eisdorfer, C. Rorschach performance and intellectual functioning in the aged. *Journal of Gerontology*, 1963, *18*, 358–363.

Ellis, A. *Reason and emotion in psychotherapy*. New York: Lyle Stuart, 1962.

Epstein, S. The self-concept revisited: Or a theory of a theory. *American Psychologist*, 1973, *28*, 404–416.

Epstein, S. Traits are alive and well. In D. Magnussan and N. S. Endler (Eds.), *Personality at the crossroads: Current issues in interactional psychology*. Hillsdale, NJ: Lawrence Erlbaum, 1977.

Epstein, S. The stability of behavior: I. On predicting most of the people much of the time. *Journal of Personality and Social Psychology*, 1979, *37*, 1097–1126.

Erikson, E. H. *Childhood and society*. New York: Norton, 1950.

Erikson, E. H. *Young man Luther: A study in psychoanalysis and history.* New York: Norton, 1962.

Eysenck, H. J. The effects of psychotherapy: An evaluation. *Journal of Consulting Psychology*, 1952, *16*, 319–324.

Eysenck, H. J. *The structure of human personality.* London: Methuen, 1960.

Eysenck, S. B. G., and Eysenck, H. J. Scores on three personality variables as a function of age, sex and social class. *British Journal of Social and Clinical Psychology*, 1969, *8*, 69–76.

Farrell, M. P., and Rosenberg, S. D. *Men at midlife.* Boston: Auburn House, 1981.

Fiske, D. W. *Strategies for personality research.* San Francisco: Jossey-Bass, 1978.

Freud, A. *The ego and the mechanisms of defense.* New York: International Universities Press, 1936.

Freud, S. *New introductory lectures in psychoanalysis*, trans. W. J. H. Sprott. New York: Norton, 1933.

Freud, S. The interpretation of dreams. In *The basic writings of Sigmund Freud.* New York: Random House, 1938.

Friedlander, J. S., Costa, P. T., Jr., Bossé, R., Ellis, E., Rhodes, J. G., and Stoudt, H. Longitudinal physique changes among healthy white veterans at Boston. *Human Biology*, 1977, *49*, 541–558.

Goffman, E. *The presentation of self in everyday life.* New York: Doubleday Anchor, 1959.

Goldberg, L. R. Language and individual differences: The search for universals in personality lexicons. In L. Wheeler (Ed.), *Review of personality and social psychology*, Vol. 2. Beverly Hills, CA: Sage, 1981.

Gough, H. G. *California psychological inventory manual.* Palo Alto, CA: Consulting Psychologists Press, 1957.

Gould, R. L. The phases of adult life: A study in developmental psychology. *American Journal of Psychiatry*, 1972, *29*, 521–531.

Gould, R. L. *Transformations.* New York: Simon and Schuster, 1978.

Guilford, J. P. *Personality.* New York: McGraw-Hill, 1959.

Guilford, J. P. Will the real factor of introversion-extraversion please stand up? A reply to Eysenck. *Psychological Bulletin*, 1977, *84*, 412–416.

Guilford, J. S., Zimmerman, W. S., and Guilford, J. P. *The Guilford-Zimmerman Temperament Survey handbook: Twenty-five years of research and application.* San Diego, CA: EdITS Publishers, 1976.

Gutmann, D. L. An exploration of ego configurations in middle and later life. In B. L. Neugarten (Ed.), *Personality in middle and later life.* New York: Atherton, 1964.

Gutmann, D. L. Female ego styles and generational conflict. In J. M. Bardwich, E. Douvan, M. S. Horner, and D. L. Gutmann (Eds.), *Feminine personality and conflict.* Belmont, CA: Brooks/Cole, 1970.

Gutmann, D. L. Alternatives to disengagement: The old men of highland Druze. In R. LeVine (Ed.), *Culture and personality: Contemporary readings.* Chicago: Aldine, 1974.

Hale, E. Your personality—you're stuck with it. *The Idaho Statesman*, June 8, 1981, Boise, ID.

Hathaway, S. R., and McKinley, J. C. *The Minnesota multiphasic personality inventory* (rev. ed.). Minneapolis: University of Minnesota Press, 1943.

Havighurst, R. J., McDonald, W. J., Maculen, L., and Mazel, J. Male social scientists: Lives after sixty. *The Gerontologist*, 1979, *19*, 55–60.

Herold, J. C. *The age of Napoleon.* New York: American Heritage, 1963.

Hogan, R. T. Of rituals, roles, cheaters, and spoilsports. *The Johns Hopkins Magazine*, 1979, *30*, 46–53.

Hogan, R. T. Socioanalytic theory of personality. In M. Page (Ed.), *Nebraska Symposium on Motivation.* Lincoln: University of Nebraska Press, 1982.

Holland, J. L. *The self-directed search: A guide to educational and vocational planning.* Palo Alto, CA: Consulting Psychologists Press, 1977.

James, W. *Principles of psychology.* New York: Holt, 1890.

Jaques, E. Death and the mid-life crisis. *International Journal of Psychoanalysis*, 1965, *46*, 502–513.

Jung, C. G. *Psychological types.* London: Routledge & Kegan Paul, 1923.

Kagan, J. *Change and continuity in infancy.* New York: Wiley, 1971.

Kagan, J., and Moss, H. A. *From birth to maturity.* New York: Wiley, 1962.

Kahana, B. The use of projective techniques in personality assessment of the aged. In I. C. Siegler, M. Storandt, and M. F. Elias (Eds.), *The clinical psychology of aging.* New York: Plenum, 1978.

Kahn, R. L., Wolfe, D. M., Quinn, R. P., Snoek, J. D., and Rosenthal, R. A. *Organizational stress: Studies in role conflict and ambiguity.* New York: Wiley, 1964.

Kausler, D. H. *Experimental psychology and human aging.* New York: Wiley, 1982.

Keehn, R. J., Goldberg, I. D., and Beebe, G. W. Twenty-four-year mortality follow-up of army veterans with disability separations for psychoneurosis in 1944. *Psychosomatic Medicine*, 1974, *36*, 27–46.

Kimmel, D. C. *Adulthood and aging.* New York: Wiley, 1974.

Kohlberg, L. From is to ought: How to commit the naturalistic fallacy and get away with it in the study of moral development. In T. Mischel (Ed.), *Cognitive development and epistemology.* New York: Academic Press, 1971.

Kramer, M., and Rednick, R. W. Epidemiological indices in the middle years. Unpublished paper, cited in O. G. Brim, Jr., Theories of the males midlife crisis. *The Counseling Psychologist*, 1976, *6*, 2–9.

Lacy, W. B., and Hendricks, J. Developmental model of adult life: Myth or reality. *International Journal of Aging and Human Development*, 1980, *11*, 89–110.

Lawton, M. P., Whelihan, W. M., and Belsky, J. K. Personality tests and their uses with older adults. In J. Birren (Ed.), *Handbook of mental health and aging.* New York: Prentice-Hall, 1980.

Lecky, P. *Self-consistency: A theory of personality.* New York: Island Press, 1945.

Leon, R. R., Gillum, B., Gillum, R., and Gouze, M. Personality stability and change over a thirty-year period—middle age to old age. *Journal of Consulting and Clinical Psychology*, 1979, *23*, 245–259.

Levinson, D. J., Darrow, C. N., Klein, E. B., Levinson, M. L., and McKee, B. *The seasons of a man's life.* New York: Knopf, 1978.

Levy, L. Trait approaches. In M. Hersen, A. E. Kazden, and A. S. Bellack (Eds.), *The clinical psychology handbook*. New York: Pergamon Press, in press.

Lieberman, M. A. Adaptive processes in late life. In N. Datan and L. H. Ginsberg (Eds.), *Life-span developmental psychology: Normative life crises*. New York: Academic Press, 1975.

Liker, J. K., and Elder, G. H. Economic pressures and family stress in the 1930's: A life course perspective on personality and family patterns. *American Sociological Review*, in press.

Livson, N. Developmental dimensions of personality: A life-span formulation. In P. B. Baltes and K. W. Schaie (Eds.), *Life-span developmental psychology: Personality and socialization*. New York: Academic Press, 1973.

Loevinger, J. The meaning and measurement of ego development. *American Psychologist*, 1966, *21*, 195–206.

Lowenthal, M. F., and Chiriboga, D. Transition to the empty nest: Crisis, challenge, or relief. *Archives of General Psychiatry*, 1972, *26*, 8–14.

Maas, H. S., and Kuypers, J. A. *From thirty to seventy*. San Francisco: Jossey-Bass, 1974.

Maddi, S. R. *Personality theories: A comparative analysis* (4th ed.). Homewood, IL: Dorsey Press, 1980.

Maddi, S. R., and Costa, P. T., Jr. *Humanism in personology: Allport, Maslow and Murray*. Chicago: Aldine, 1972.

Maddox, G. L. Persistence of life style among the elderly: A longitudinal study of patterns of social activity in relation to life satisfaction. In B. L. Neugarten (Ed.), *Middle age and aging: A reader in social psychology*. Chicago: University of Chicago Press, 1968.

Maslow, A. H. *Motivation and personality*. New York: Harper & Row, 1954.

McClelland, D. C. Motive dispositions: The merits of operant and respondent measures. In L. Wheeler (Ed.), *Review of personality and social psychology*. Beverly Hills, CA: Sage, 1980.

McCrae, R. R. Age differences in the use of coping mechanisms. *Journal of Gerontology*, 1982, *37*, 454–460. (a)

McCrae, R. R. Consensual validation of personality traits: Evidence from self-reports and ratings. *Journal of Personality and Social Psychology*, 1982, *43*, 293–303. (b)

McCrae, R. R., and Costa, P. T., Jr. Openness to experience and ego level in Loevinger's sentence completion test: Dispositional contributions to developmental models of personality. *Journal of Personality and Social Psychology*, 1980, *39*, 1179–1190.

McCrae, R. R., and Costa, P. T., Jr. The self-concept and the stability of personality: Cross-sectional comparisons of self-reports and ratings. *Journal of Personality and Social Psychology*, 1982, *43*, 1282–1292.

McCrae, R. R., and Costa, P. T., Jr. Psychological maturity and subjective well-being: Toward a new synthesis. *Developmental Psychology*, 1983, *19*, 243–248.

McGowan, J., and Gormly, J. Validation of personality traits: A multi-criteria approach. *Journal of Personality and Social Psychology*, 1976, *34*, 791–795.

Mead, G. H. *Mind, self and society*. Chicago: University of Chicago Press, 1934.

Mortimer, J. T., Finch, M. D., and Kumka, D. Persistence and change in development: The multidimensional self-concept. In P. B. Baltes and O. G. Brim, Jr. (Eds.), *Life-span development and behavior*, Vol. IV. New York: Academic Press, 1981.

Murray, H. A. *Explorations in personality*. New York: Oxford University Press, 1938.

Murray, H. A., and Kluckhohn, C. Outline of a conception of personality. In C. Kluckhohn and H. A. Murray (Eds.), *Personality in nature, society, and culture* (2nd ed.). New York: Knopf, 1953.

Mussen, P., Eichorn, D. H., Honzik, M. P., Bieber, S. L., and Meredith, W. M. Continuity and change in women's characteristics over four decades. *International Journal of Behavioral Development*, 1980, *3*, 333–347.

Myerhoff, B. G., and Simić, A. (Eds.). *Life's career—aging: Cultural variations on growing old*. Beverly Hills, CA: Sage, 1978.

Neill, A. S. *Summerhill: A radical approach to child-rearing*. New York: Pocket Books, 1977.

Neugarten, B. L. Summary and implications. In B. L. Neugarten (Ed.), *Personality in middle and late life*. New York: Atherton, 1964.

Neugarten, B. L. (Ed.). *Middle age and aging*. Chicago: University of Chicago Press, 1968.

Neugarten, B. L. Personality and aging. In J. E. Birren and K. W. Schaie (Eds.), *Handbook of the psychology of aging*. New York: Van Nostrand Reinhold, 1977.

Peatman, J. G. *Descriptive and sampling statistics*. New York: Harper, 1947.

Reichard, S., Livson, F., and Peterson, P. G. *Aging and personality*. New York: Wiley, 1962.

Robins, L. N. *Deviant children grown up*. Baltimore: Williams & Wilkins, 1966.

Rogers, C. R. *On becoming a person: A therapist's view of psychotherapy*. Boston: Houghton Mifflin, 1961.

Rogers, C. R., and Dymond, R. F. (Eds.). *Psychotherapy and personality change*. Chicago: University of Chicago Press, 1954.

Rokeach, M. *The open and closed mind*. New York: Basic Books, 1960.

Rosenberg, M. *Conceiving the self*. New York: Basic Books, 1979.

Rotter, J. B., and Rafferty, J. E. *Manual: The Rotter incomplete sentences blank*. New York: The Psychological Corporation, 1950.

Rubin, Z. Does personality really change after 20? *Psychology Today*, 1981, *15*, 18–27.

Runyan, W. McK. Why did Van Gogh cut off his ear? The problem of alternative explanations in psychobiography. *Journal of Personality and Social Psychology*, 1981, *40*, 1070–1077.

Schaie, K. W. Quasi-experimental research designs in the psychology of aging. In J. E. Birren and K. W. Schaie (Eds.), *Handbook of the psychology of aging*. New York: Van Nostrand Reinhold, 1977.

Schaie, K. W., and Labouvie-Vief, G. Generational vs. ontogenetic components of change in adult cognitive behavior: A fourteen-year cross-sequential study. *Developmental Psychology*, 1974, *10*, 305–320.

Schaie, K. W., and Parham, I. Stability of adult personality traits: Fact or fable? *Journal of Personality and Social Psychology*, 1976, *34*, 146–158.

Schweder, R. A. How relevant is an individual difference theory of personality? *Journal of Personality*, 1975, *43*, 455–484.

Sheehy, G. *Passages: Predictable crises of adult life*. New York: Dutton, 1976.

Siegler, I. C., George, L. K., and Okun, M. A. Cross-sequential analysis of adult personality. *Developmental Psychology*, 1979, *15*, 350–351.

Skinner, B. F. Intellectual self-management in old age. *American Psychologist*, 1983, *38*, 239–244.

Skolnick, A. Stability and interrelationships of thematic test imagery over twenty years. *Child Development*, 1966, *37*, 389–396.

Small, S. A., Zeldin, R. S., and Savin-Williams, R. C. In search of personality traits: A multimethod analysis of naturally occurring prosocial and dominance behavior. *Journal of Personality*, 1983, *51*, 1–16.

Spock, B. *Baby and child care*. New York: Pocket Books, 1946.

Strong, E. K., Jr. *Vocational interests 18 years after college*. Minneapolis: University of Minnesota Press, 1955.

Stuart, R. B. (Ed.). *Behavioral self-management*. New York: Brunner/Mazel, 1977.

Suinn, R. M., and Oskamp, S. *The predictive validity of projective measures: A fifteen-year evaluative review of research*. Springfield, IL: Charles C Thomas, 1969.

Swann, W. B., Jr. Self-verification: Bringing social reality into harmony with the self. In J. Suls and A. G. Greenwald (Eds.), *Psychological perspectives on the self*, Vol. 2. Hillsdale, NJ: Erlbaum, in press.

Swann, W. B., Jr., and Hill, C. A. When our identities are mistaken: Reaffirming self-conceptions through social interactions. *Journal of Personality and Social Psychology*, 1982, *43*, 59–66.

Tamir, L. M. *Men in their forties: The transition to middle age*. New York: Springer, 1982.

Tellegen, A., and Atkinson, G. Openness to absorbing and self-altering experiences ("absorption"), a trait related to hypnotic susceptibility. *Journal of Abnormal Psychology*, 1974, *83*, 268–277.

Thomas, A., Chess, S., and Birch, H. G. *Temperament and behavior disorders in children*. New York: New York University Press, 1968.

Troll, L. E., Miller, S. J., and Atchley, R. C. *Families in later life*. Belmont, CA: Wadsworth, 1979.

Tsuang, M. T., Woolson, R. F., Winokur, G., and Crowe, R. R. Stability of psychiatric diagnosis: Schizophrenia and affection disorders followed up over a 30- to 40-year period. *Archives of General Psychiatry*, 1981, *38*, 535–539.

Vaillant, G. E. *Adaptation to life*. Boston: Little, Brown, 1977.

Veroff, J., Atkinson, J. W., Feld, S. C., and Gurin, G. The use of thematic apperception to assess motivation in a nationwide interview study. *Psychological Monographs*, 1960, *74* (12, Whole No. 499).

Werner, H. The concept of development from a comparative and organismic view. In D. B. Harris (Ed.), *The concept of development*. Minneapolis: University of Minnesota Press, 1957.

Whitbourne, S. K., and Waterman, A. S. Psychosocial development during the adult years: Age and cohort comparisons. *Developmental Psychology*, 1979, *15*, 373–378.

White, R. W. *Lives in progress: A study of the natural growth of personality.* New York: Holt, Rinehart and Winston, 1952.

Winter, D. G., and Stewart, A. Power motive reliability as a function of retest instructions. *Journal of Consulting and Clinical Psychology,* 1977, *45,* 436–440.

Witkin, H. A., Dyk, R. B., Paterson, H. F., Goodenough, D. R., and Karp, S. A. *Psychological differentiation.* New York: Wiley, 1962

Woodruff, D. The role of memory in personality continuity: A 25 year follow-up. *Experimental Aging Research,* 1983, *9,* 31–34.

Woodruff, D. S., and Birren, J. E. Age changes and cohort differences in personality. *Developmental Psychology,* 1972, *6,* 252–259.

Young, P. A., Eaves, L. J., and Eysenck, H. J. Intergenerational stability and change in the causes of variation in personality. *Personality and Individual Differences,* 1980, *1,* 35–56.

Zuckerman, M. *Sensation seeking: Beyond the optimal level of arousal.* New York: Lawrence Erlbaum, 1979.

Index